Process selection
From design to manufacture

K G Swift
Lucas Professor of Manufacturing Systems Engineering
Department of Engineering Design and Manufacture
University of Hull

J D Booker
Research Associate
Department of Engineering Design and Manufacture
University of Hull

A member of the Hodder Headline Group
LONDON • SYDNEY • AUCKLAND
Copublished in North, Central and South America by
John Wiley & Sons Inc., New York • Toronto

Published in Great Britain in 1997 by
Arnold, a member of the Hodder Headline Group
338 Euston Road, London NW1 3BH

Copublished in North, Central and South America by
John Wiley & Sons, Inc., 605 Third Avenue,
New York, NY 10158-0012

British Library Cataloguing in Publication Data
A catalogue record for this book is available from the British Library

Library of Congress Cataloging-in-Publication Data
A catalog record for this book is available from the Library of Congress

ISBN 0 340 69249 9
ISBN 0 470 23774 0 (Wiley)

Typeset in Times and Univers. Produced by Gray Publishing, Tunbridge Wells, Kent
Printed and bound in Great Britain by JW Arrowsmith, Bristol

Contents

Preface

In order to facilitate the achievement of the required quality and cost objectives for the manufacture of a component design solution it is necessary to carry out the interrelated activities of selecting candidate processes and tuning a design to get the best out of a chosen manufacturing route. These are difficult decision-making tasks that few experts do well, particularly in the situation of new product introduction.

Failure to get this right often results in late engineering change, with its associated problems of high cost and lead time protraction, or having to live with components that are of poor quality and/or expensive to make.

There is a need for specialist knowledge across a range of manufacturing technologies to enable the correct design decisions to be made from the breadth of possibilities. The difficulties faced by businesses in this area are frequently due to a lack of the necessary detailed knowledge and the absence of process selection methods.

The main motivation behind the text is the provision of technological and economic data on a range of important manufacturing processes. Manufacturing **PR**ocess Information **MA**ps (PRIMAs) provide detailed data on the characteristics and capabilities of each process in a standard format under headings including: material suitability, design considerations, quality issues, general economics and process fundamentals and variations. A distinctive feature is the inclusion of process tolerance capability charts for processing key material types.

Another distinctive feature of the book is the inclusion of a method for estimating component costs, based on both design characteristics and manufacturing process routes. The cost associated with processing a design is based on the notion of a design independent basic processing cost and a set of relative cost coefficients for taking account of the design application including geometry and tolerances, etc. The overall component cost is logically based on the sum of the material processing and material purchase cost elements. While the method was primarily designed for use with company specific data, approximate data on a sample of common manufacturing processes and material groups is included to illustrate the design costing process and quantify the effect of design choices and alternative process routes on manufacturing cost.

The work is presented in three main parts. Part I addresses the background to the problem and puts process selection and costing into the context of modern product introduction processes and the application of techniques in design for manufacture. Part II presents the manufacturing process information maps (PRIMAs) and their selection. Part III is concerned with methods and data for costing design solutions.

The book is primarily intended to be useful to engineering businesses as an aid to the problem of selecting processes and costing design alternatives in the context of concurrent engineering. The work will also be useful as an introduction to manufacturing processes and their selection for all students of design, technology and management.

The authors are very grateful to Liz Davidson of CMB Ltd, for her efforts in collecting data on many of the processes included, and to Robert Braund of T&N Ltd, for his contribution to extending the data sheets and particularly for his work on the effects of component section thickness and size on process selection and costing. The authors are also greatly indebted to Adrian Allen of Chaumont Ltd, for his valuable contribution to the research at Hull concerned with methodologies for manufacturing process selection and costing.

Thanks are also due to Phil Baker, Graham Hird, Duncan Law and Brian Miles of CSC Manufacturing Ltd, (formerly Lucas Engineering & Systems Ltd) for their encouragement and enthusiastic support, and to Bob Swain of the University of Hull for help with manuscript preparation.

The Engineering and Physical Sciences Research Council (EPSRC) of the UK is gratefully acknowledged for support (under research grant number GR/J97922) for research concerned with process capability and design costing.

K G Swift and J D Booker
Department of Engineering Design and Manufacture,
University of Hull

Notation

List of terms

Cc	relative cost associated with producing components of different geometrical complexity
Cf	relative cost associated with obtaining a specified surface finish
Cft	value of Ct or Cf (whichever is greatest)
Cmp	relative cost associated with material-process suitability
Cmt	cost of the material per unit volume in the required form
Cs	relative cost associated with size considerations and achieving component section reductions/thickness
Ct	relative cost associated with obtaining a specified tolerance
Mc	material cost
Mi	manufacturing cost (pence)
n	number of operations required to achieve the finished component
N	total component demand
Pc	basic processing cost for an ideal design of component by a specific process
Ra	roughness average
Rc	relative cost coefficient assigned to a component design
T	process time in seconds for processing an ideal design of component by a specific process
V	volume of material required in order to produce the component
Vf	finished volume of the component
Wc	waste coefficient
α	cost of setting up and operating a specific process, including plant, labour, supervision and overheads, per second
β	process specific total tooling cost for an ideal design

Acronyms used

DFA	Design for Assembly
DFM	Design for Manufacture
DOE	Design of Experiments
FMEA	Failure Mode and Effects Analysis
PIM	Product Introduction Management
PRIMA	Process Information Map
QFD	Quality Function Deployment

Units (SI)

m	=	metre
μm	=	micron (micrometre)
mm	=	millimetre
cm	=	centimetre
kg	=	kilogramme
g	=	gramme
t	=	tonne
min	=	minute

Part I
A strategic view

Some background to the problem, and placing manufacturing process selection and costing into the context of modern product introduction and the application of techniques in design for manufacture.

1.1 The problem

Fierce competition and higher customer expectations are forcing manufacturing business-es to improve quality, lower selling prices, and shorten time to market. This all places new pressures on the product introduction process.

Consequently, there is a realization in the manufacturing industry that increasing man-ufacturing efficiency, improving quality and reducing costs does not only accrue from investment in automation and advanced machine tools. Selecting the most appropriate manufacturing process in terms of technological feasibility and cost for a component design is one of the most important decision-making tasks: failure to get it right normally results in components that are of variable quality and/or expensive to make.

In order to take full advantage of a manufacturing process, whether old or new, it is nec-essary to ensure, where possible, that the component design can be manufactured most efficiently and economically by the chosen technology. This aspect is part of product design and clearly if this is to be realized the designer must be aware of the manufactur-ing route by which a component is produced. In most cases it is found that there are a num-ber of manufacturing processes that can be used for the component, and the selection of the most appropriate process depends upon a large number of factors. This is not a sim-ple problem. Its solution requires considerable manufacturing expertise and there are a lack of systematic techniques to assist the designer in this area.

1.2 Manufacturing information for design

The need to provide the design activity with information regarding manufacturing process capabilities and costs has been recognized for many years (1.1) and some of the work that has been done to address this problem will be touched on below.

There is relatively little published work in this area; the books on design rarely include relevant data and while a few of the volumes on manufacturing processes do provide some aid in terms of process selection and costs (1.2–1.6), the information is not sufficiently detailed and systematically presented to do more than indicate the apparent enormity of the problem.

Typically, the facts tend to be process specific and described in different formats in each case, making the engineer's task more difficult. There is a considerable amount of data available, but precious little knowledge of how this can be applied to the problem of man-ufacturing process selection.

The available information tends to be inconsistent: some processes are described in great detail, while others are perhaps neglected. This may give a disproportionate impres-sion of the processes and their availability.

Information can also be found displayed in a tabulated and comparative form on the basis of specific process criteria (1.2, 1.3). While useful, the design-related data tend to be limited and no, or very little, detailed data are included. Such forms may be adequate if the designer has expertise in the respective processes, but otherwise gaps in the detail leave room for misconceptions and may be a poor foundation for decision making.

Manufacturing catalogues and information can be helpful, however, they tend to be sales oriented and again, data are presented in different formats and at various levels of detail. Suppliers rarely provide much on design considerations or information on process capability. In addition, there are often differences in language between the process experts and the users.

In recent years a number of research groups have concentrated specifically on the design/manufacture interface; processes and systems for cost estimation are under development in areas including machining (1.7), powder metallurgy (1.8), die casting (1.9) and on broader techniques with the goal of providing DFM (design for manufacture) and cost-related information for the designer (1.10–1.14).

A review of cost-estimation techniques for the early stages of design and a method for relating product cost to material cost, total batch size and level of underlying technology can be found in reference (1.15).

Companies recognizing the importance of design for manufacture have also searched for many years for a solution to this problem with most opting for some kind of product 'team' approach, involving a multitude of persons supposedly providing the necessary breadth of experience in order to obtain 'production-friendly products'. While sometimes obtaining reasonable results, this approach often faces a number of obstacles: assembling a team with the relevant experience; lack of formal structure – typically such meetings tend to be unstructured and often *ad hoc* attacks on various 'pet' themes; the location of the persons required in the team can also present problems – not only are designers and production engineers found in different functional departments, but they can frequently be on different sites and, in the case of sub-contractors, in different companies. In addition, the chances are that the expertise in the team will only cover the primary activities of the business and hence opportunity to exploit any benefits from alternative processes may be lost.

The greatest opportunity in design for manufacture occurs at the initial design stage, for while there are also possibilities when a product in production is to be modified, there are many additional constraints. This is illustrated in Figure 1.1. On top of the problems of tooling and equipment it is not uncommon to find that the 'ownership' of a design changes many times. Consequently the logic behind a design can become clouded, with the result that subsequent 'owners' tend to assume that existing features must be there for good reason and resist change, even though in fact there may be great opportunities for cost reductions.

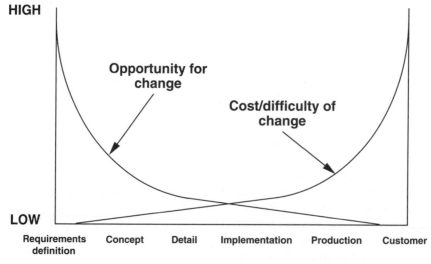

Figure 1.1 Opportunity for change during the early stages of product introduction

The traditional, functionally organized product introduction process is incapable of meeting the new pressures placed upon it. Its problems are summarized below:

- Sequential activity results in protracted lead times

- Customer requirements, product design and method of manufacture are inextricably linked with many tradeoffs: they cannot be addressed independently by marketing, engineering and manufacturing functions

- Scarce design resources are wasted on interdepartmental communications, progress chasing and non-value added activities correcting designs that prove difficult to make or do not fully meet customer's requirements

- Manufacturability issues are discovered too late and are the subject of quick-fix solutions and compromises

- All design activity is pushed through a single, ill-defined activity

- Products are designed with an excessive number of component parts which in addition to the cost of these parts adds to the cost of supply and stock control.

Figure 1.2   Problems of the traditional approach to product introduction

Some companies do have a structured/formal approach to design ownership and alterations, however, these are not always sufficiently annotated. The problems associated with the traditional, functionally organized product introduction process are summarized in Figure 1.2 (1.16).

1.3   Product introduction processes

Faced with the above issues, some companies are currently making dramatic changes to the way in which products are brought to market. The traditional engineering-function-led sequential product introduction process is being replaced by a faster and far more effective team-based simultaneous engineering approach (1.16).

For example, the need for change has been recognized in Lucas Industries and has led to the development of a product introduction management (PIM) process (1.17) for use in all Lucas businesses with the declared target of reducing:

- time to market by 30%
- product cost by 20%
- project cost by 30%.

The generic process is characterized by five phases and nine reviews as indicated in Figure 1.3. Each review has a relevant set of commercial, technical and project criteria for sign-off and hand-over to the next stage.

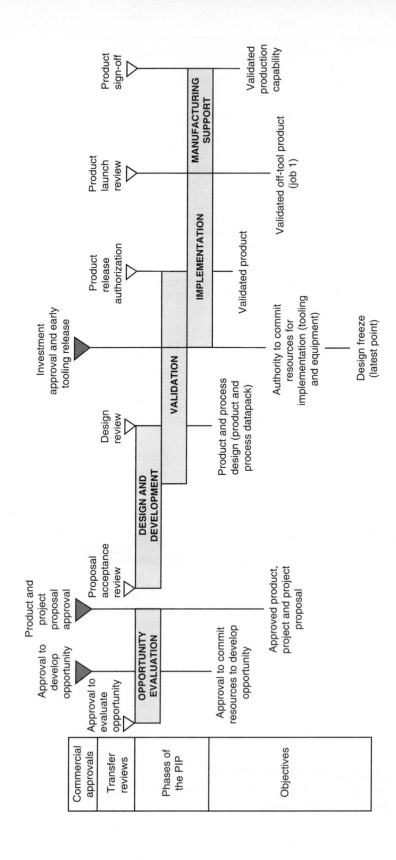

Figure 1.3 The Lucas product introduction management (PIM) process

To be effective, product introduction requires the collaborative use of:

- Teamwork – product development undertaken by a full-time co-located team with representation from marketing, product development engineering, manufacturing systems engineering, manufacturing, suppliers and customers formed at the requirements definition stage and selected for team-working and technical skills.
- Simultaneous engineering – the simultaneous design of product, its method of manufacture and, the manufacturing system, against clear customer requirements at equal levels of product and process definition.
- Project management – the professional management of every product introduction project against clearly defined and agreed cost, quality and delivery targets specified to achieve complete customer satisfaction and business profitability.
- Tools and techniques – the routine use of concurrent engineering tools to structure the team's activity, thereby improving the productivity of the team and quality of their output.

The linkage between the above elements is represented diagrammatically in Figure 1.4.

Design for assembly (DFA) is one of the main tools and techniques prescribed by the PIM process. (Other main tools and techniques currently specified include: quality function deployment (QFD) (1.18), failure mode and effects analysis (FMEA) (1.19) and design of experiments (DOE) (1.20).)

Significant benefits have been obtained through the use of the tools and techniques in a team-based simultaneous engineering environment. They inject method, objectivity and structured continuous feedback, and improve a team's communication and understanding.

Impressive results have been produced in businesses world-wide by the application of techniques in DFA. A review of 40 DFA studies (1.16) using Lucas DFA in the aerospace, automotive and industrial product sectors shows an average part-count reduction of 46% and an average assembly cost reduction of 47%. Implemented unit cost savings on direct labour and material costs only are reported in the range 15–35%. It is interesting to note

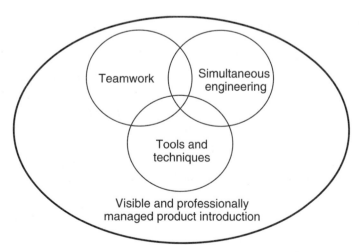

Figure 1.4   Key elements of successful product introduction

that these benefits were achieved on top of what were considered as good team designs with value analysis (1.21). Similar savings have been reported by others involved in the application of DFA (1.22).

DFA techniques (1.23–1.25) are capable of identifying opportunities for part-count reduction and potential costs of manufacture and assembly. The analysis metrics associated with part count and potential costs are inputs to concept design and development. As part of the DFA process the product development team needs to generate improved product design solutions, with better DFA metrics, by simplifying the product structure, reducing part count and simplifying component assembly operations.

DFA is particularly interesting in the context of this book since its main benefits result from systematically reviewing functional requirements and replacing component clusters by single integrated pieces (1.26, 1.27). Invariably the proposed design solutions rely heavily on the viability of adopting different manufacturing processes and/or materials (see Figure 1.5).

As mentioned previously, selecting the correct manufacturing process is not always simple and obvious. In most cases there are several processes that can be used for a component and selection depends on a large number of factors. Some of the process selection drivers are:

- Product quantity.
- Equipment costs.
- Tooling costs.
- Processing times.
- Labour intensity and work patterns.
- Process supervision.
- Maintenance.
- Energy consumption and other overhead costs.
- Material costs and availability.
- Material to process compatibility.
- Component form and dimensions.
- Tolerance requirements.
- Surface finish needs.
- Bulk treatment and surface engineering.
- Process to component variability.
- Process waste.
- Component recycling.

The intention is not to infer that these are necessarily of equal importance or occur in this fixed sequence.

The problem is compounded by the range of manufacturing processes and material types commonly in use. Figures 1.6 and 1.7 provide a general classification and guide to the range of materials and manufacturing processes that are widely available.

To be competitive, the identification of technologically and economically feasible manufacturing process and material combinations are crucial. The benefits of picking the right process can be enormous (see Figure 1.8).

The placing in the design cycle of process selection and detail design for minimum manufacturing cost is represented in Figure 1.9, taken from reference (1.28). According to Boothroyd *et al.*, the figure summarizes the steps taken when using DFMA (design for manufacture and assembly) during design. It suggests that DFA is used first to simplify the

Example 1

After (1.26)

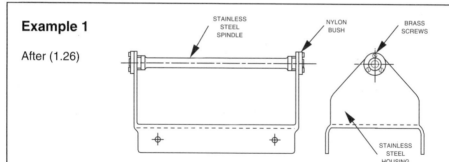

This spindle/housing assembly (sheet metal housing) has ten separate parts and an assembly efficiency rating of 7%.

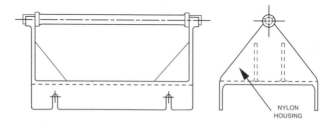

The two part design, utilising an injection-moulded nylon housing, has an assembly efficiency rating of 93%.

Example 2

After (1.27)

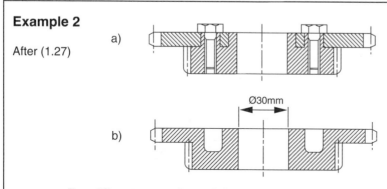

Two different types of sprocket and gear wheel: (a) includes assembly: this is made of steel and produced by machining. The individual teeth are cut. It is necessary to divide it in to two elements due to production technique reasons. (b) does not include assembly: this is produced from sintered metal, the teeth being sintered in accordance with the required tolerance and surface quality; the advantages being no waste material, short processing time and no assembly.

Figure 1.5 Examples of part-count reduction

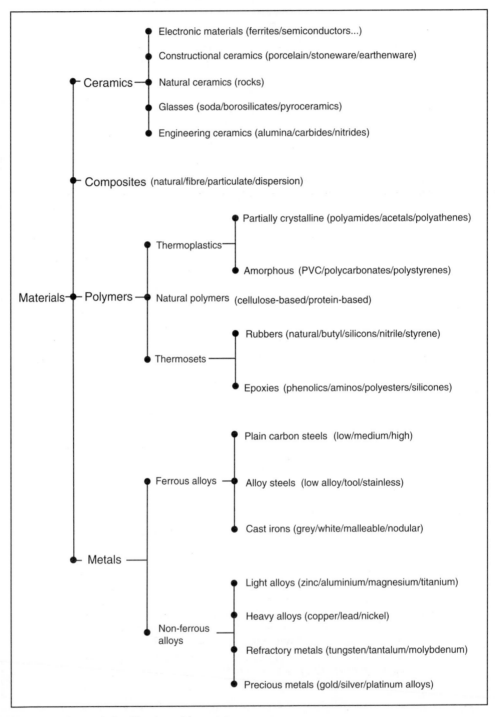

Figure 1.6 General classification of materials

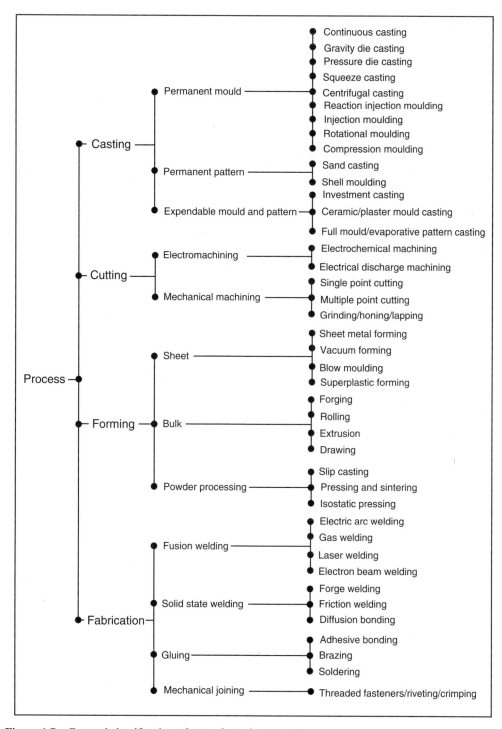

Figure 1.7   General classification of manufacturing processes

Component	Material	Number Per Annum	Manufacturing Process	Relative Cost
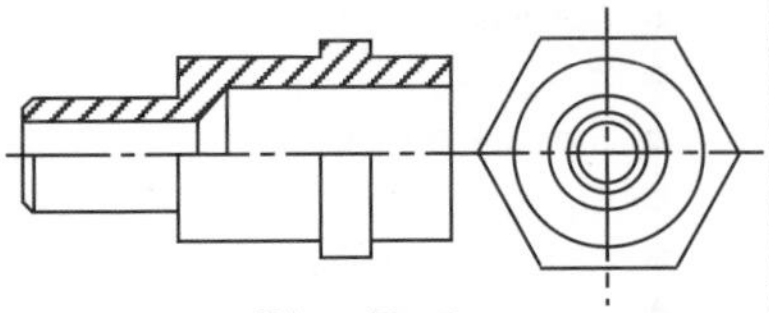 Plug Body	Low Carbon Steel	1,000,000	Machining	4.1
			Cold Forming	1
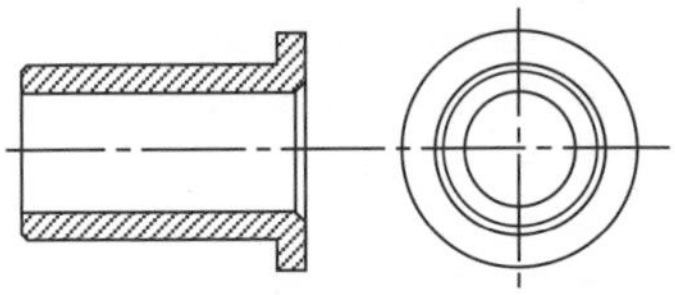 Plain Bearing	Bronze	50,000	Machining	2.2
			Powder Metal Sintering	1
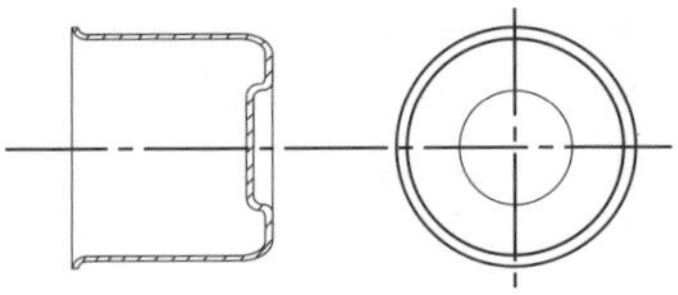 Cover	Aluminium Alloy	5,000	Spinning	1.8
			Deep Drawing	1
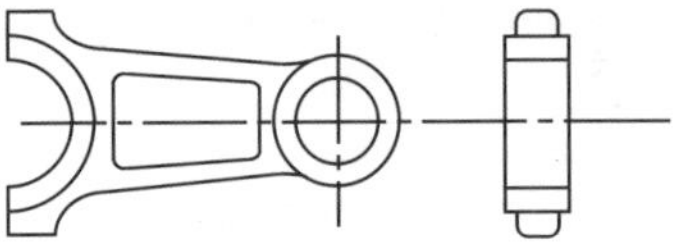 Connecting Rod*	Medium Carbon Steel	100,000	Closed Die Forging	1.3
			Sand Casting	1
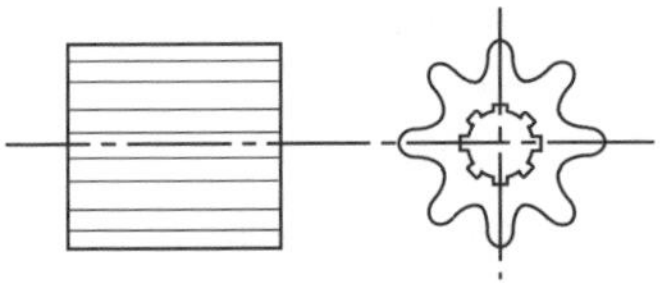 Pump Gear	Low Carbon Steel	500	Machining	2.6
			Cold Extrusion	1

*Ref. (1.30)

Figure 1.8 Contrast in component cost for different processing routes

product structure to get the right part count. This is followed by obtaining early cost estimates for parts in both the original and new design solution to facilitate trade-off decisions. It is proposed that during the activity the best material to process combinations are considered. Having selected the most appropriate materials and processes a more thorough analysis for DFM is advocated.

In Figure 1.9 the term DFM is used in the context of detail design for processing. DFM is often taken to have a wider meaning (1.29–1.31), with DFA being but a part of this broader definition. However, this should not cloud the issue and the diagram is believed to represent a good approach to the practical application of data, knowledge and

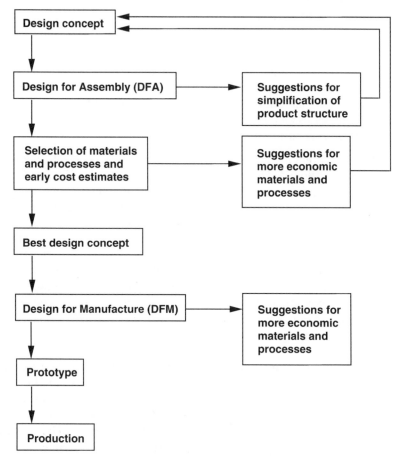

Figure 1.9   Typical steps taken in simultaneous engineering study using DFMA techniques (1.28)

methods associated with manufacturing process selection and design for minimum manufacturing cost.

A reader interested in more background on manufacturing processes and their selection in product introduction is referred to references (1.32–1.35).

1.4   A process selection strategy

In considering alternative design solutions for cost and quality, it is necessary to explore candidate materials, geometries and tolerances, etc., against possible manufacturing routes. This requires some means of selecting appropriate processes and estimating the costs of manufacture early on in product development, across a whole range of options. In addition, the costs of non-conformance (1.36) need to be understood, that is appraisal (inspection and testing) and failure, both internal (rework, etc.) and external (customer returns, warranty claims, liability and recall, etc.) Therefore, we also need a way of exploring conformance levels before a process is selected.

The primary objective of the text is to provide support for manufacturing process selection in terms of technological feasibility, quality of conformance and manufacturing cost. The satisfaction of this objective is through:

- the provision of data on the characteristics and capabilities of a range of important manufacturing processes. The intention is to promote the generation of design ideas and facilitate the matching and tuning of a design to a process, and
- the provision of methods and data to enable the exploration of component design solutions for manufacturing cost in the early stages of the design process.

To provide for the first point a set of so-called manufacturing process information maps or PRIMAs have been developed. The PRIMAs present, in a standard format for each process, knowledge and data on areas including: material suitability, design considerations, quality of conformance, economics and process fundamentals and variations.

The information includes not only design considerations relevant for the respective processes, but quite purposefully, an overview of the functional characteristics of the process so that a greater overall understanding may be achieved.

Within the standard format a similar level of detail is provided on each of the processes included. The format is very deliberate. First, an outline of the process itself – how it works and under what conditions it functions best. Secondly, a summary of what it can do – limitations and opportunities it presents, and finally, an overview of quality considerations including process capability charts for relating tolerances to characteristic dimensions.

To provide for the second point, a technique is put forward that can be used to estimate the costs of component manufacture for concept designs. It enables the effects of design geometry and materials to be explored against various manufacturing routes.

A sample data set is included which enables the technique to be used to predict component manufacturing costs for a range of processes and materials. The process of cost estimation is illustrated through a number of case studies and the scope for and importance of application with company specific data is discussed.

The body of the text begins in Part II with a guide to PRIMA selection, where attention is focused on candidate processes based on material and production quantity. Five main groups of component manufacturing processes are considered: casting, plastic and composite processing methods, forming, machining and non-traditional processes. In addition, 10 fabrication and joining processes are included. In all, nearly 50 PRIMAs are presented.

Part III of the text concentrates on the cost estimation methodology, its background, theoretical development and industrial application.

In practice, Part II of the work can be used to help select the candidate processes for a design from the whole range of possibilities. Part III is concerned with getting a feel for the manufacturing cost of the alternatives.

The book finishes with a statement of conclusions and a list of areas where future work might be usefully directed.

Part II
Selecting candidate processes

Information and data relevant to selecting candidate manufacturing processes for design solutions.

2.1 Introduction

Selecting the right process and optimizing the design to suit the process selected involves a series of decisions which exert considerable influence on the quality and cost of components and assemblies. Such decisions can significantly effect the success of a product in the market place.

As mentioned previously, in selecting processes and tuning designs for processing many factors need to be taken into consideration. The manufacturing process information maps (PRIMAs) presented in this part of the book attempt to provide the knowledge and data required to underpin this decision-making process.

A method is provided for selecting the most appropriate manufacturing processes. The PRIMAs provide the means of making more detailed assessments regarding the technological and economic feasibility of a process.

Design considerations are provided to enable the designer to understand more about those design aspects which are important to technical feasibility and cost of a process. The process quality considerations give the designer valuable information on process conformance, including data on process tolerance capability associated with characteristic dimensions.

A good proportion of the PRIMAs is taken up with quality considerations. No excuse is made for this. Non-conformance often represents a large quality cost in a business. As touched on earlier, such losses result from rework, order exchange, warranty claims, legal actions and recall. In many businesses these losses account for more than 10% of turnover (2.1).

The goal is to provide data which enables the selection of processes that have the capability to satisfy the engineering needs of the application, including those associated with conformance to quality requirements.

2.2 PRIMA selection

The purpose of this section is to provide a general guide as to what processes may be suitable targets for a component. The manufacturing process selection strategy is given below:

1. obtain an estimate of the annual production quantity
2. choose a material type to satisfy the product design specification
3. refer to Figure 2.1 to select candidate PRIMAs
4. consider each PRIMA against the engineering and economic requirements:
   - understand the process and its variations
   - consider the material compatibility
   - assess conformance of component concept with design rules
   - compare tolerance and surface finish requirements with process capability data
5. consider the economic positioning of the process and obtain component cost estimates for alternatives
6. review the selected manufacturing process against business requirements.

The principal intention is that the candidate processes are selected before the component design is finalized, so that any specific constraints and/or opportunities may be borne in mind.

Note - The PRIMA selection matrix cannot be regarded as comprehensive and should not be taken as such. It represents the main common industrial practice but there will always be exceptions at this level of detail. Also, the order in which the PRIMAs are listed in the nodes of the matrix has no significance in terms of preference.

MATERIAL → / QUANTITY ↓	IRONS	STEEL (carbon)	STEEL (tool, alloy)	STAINLESS STEEL	COPPER & ALLOYS	ALUMINIUM & ALLOYS	MAGNESIUM & ALLOYS	ZINC & ALLOYS	TIN & ALLOYS	LEAD & ALLOYS	NICKEL & ALLOYS	TITANIUM & ALLOYS	THERMOPLASTICS	THERMOSETS	FR COMPOSITES	CERAMICS	REACTIVE METALS	PRECIOUS METALS
VERY SMALL 1 TO 100	[1.5] [1.6] [1.7] [4.M]	[1.5] [1.7] [3.6] [4.M] [5.1] [5.5] [5.6]	[1.1] [1.7] [3.6] [4.M] [5.1] [5.5] [5.6]	[1.7] [3.6] [4.M] [5.1] [5.5] [5.6]	[1.5] [1.7] [3.6] [4.M] [5.1]	[1.5] [1.7] [3.6] [4.M] [5.1] [5.5]	[1.6] [1.7] [3.6] [4.M] [5.1] [5.5]	[1.1] [1.7] [3.6] [4.M] [5.5]	[1.1] [1.7] [3.6] [4.M] [5.5]	[1.1] [3.6] [4.M] [5.5]	[1.5] [1.7] [3.6] [4.M] [5.1] [5.5] [5.6]	[1.1] [1.6] [4.M] [5.1] [5.5] [5.6]	[2.3] [2.5]		[2.6]	[5.6]		[5.5]
SMALL 100 TO 1,000	[1.2] [1.3] [1.5] [1.7] [4.M] [5.3] [5.4]	[1.2] [1.3] [1.5] [1.7] [3.6] [4.M] [5.1] [5.3] [5.4] [5.5]	[1.1] [1.7] [3.6] [4.M] [5.1] [5.3] [5.4] [5.5] [5.6]	[1.2] [1.7] [3.6] [4.M] [5.1] [5.3] [5.4] [5.5]	[1.2] [1.3] [1.5] [1.7] [1.8] [3.3] [3.6] [4.M] [5.1] [5.3] [5.4]	[1.2] [1.3] [1.5] [1.7] [1.8] [3.6] [4.M] [5.3] [5.4] [5.5]	[1.3] [1.6] [1.7] [1.8] [3.6] [4.M] [5.5]	[1.1] [1.3] [1.7] [1.8] [3.6] [4.M] [5.5]	[1.1] [1.3] [1.7] [1.8] [3.6] [4.M] [5.5]	[1.1] [1.3] [1.8] [3.6] [4.M] [5.5]	[1.2] [1.3] [1.5] [1.7] [3.6] [4.M] [5.1] [5.3] [5.4] [5.5]	[1.1] [1.6] [4.M] [5.3] [5.4] [5.5] [5.6]	[2.2] [2.3] [2.5]	[2.2]	[2.2] [2.6]	[5.6]		[5.5]
SMALL TO MEDIUM 1,000 TO 10,000	[1.2] [1.3] [1.5] [1.7] [3.7] [4.A] [5.2]	[1.2] [1.3] [1.5] [1.7] [3.1] [3.2] [3.7] [4.A] [5.2] [5.3] [5.4] [5.5]	[1.2] [1.7] [3.1] [3.2] [3.7] [4.A] [5.2] [5.3] [5.4] [5.5]	[1.2] [1.7] [3.1] [3.2] [3.7] [4.A] [5.2] [5.3] [5.4] [5.5]	[1.2] [1.3] [1.4] [1.5] [1.8] [3.1] [3.2] [5.2] [5.3] [5.4]	[1.2] [1.3] [1.4] [1.5] [1.8] [3.1] [3.2] [4.A] [5.4] [5.5]	[1.3] [1.4] [1.6] [1.8] [3.1] [3.2] [4.A] [5.5]	[1.3] [1.4] [1.8] [3.2] [4.A] [5.5]	[1.3] [1.4] [3.2]	[1.3] [1.4] [3.2]	[1.2] [1.3] [1.5] [1.7] [3.1] [3.2] [3.7] [4.A] [5.2] [5.3] [5.4] [5.5]	[3.1] [3.7] [4.A] [5.2] [5.3] [5.4] [5.5]	[2.1] [2.2] [2.3] [2.4]	[2.2]	[2.2]	[5.2]		[5.5]
MEDIUM TO HIGH 10,000 TO 100,000	[1.2] [1.3] [3.7] [4.A]	[3.1] [3.2] [3.3] [3.8] [4.A] [5.5]	[3.2] [3.3] [3.8] [4.A] [5.2]	[3.1] [3.2] [3.3] [3.7] [3.8] [4.A]	[3.2] [3.3] [3.7] [3.8] [4.A]	[3.1] [3.2] [3.3] [3.7] [3.8] [4.A] [5.5]	[1.3] [1.4] [3.1] [3.2] [3.3] [3.8] [4.A]	[1.4] [3.2] [3.8] [4.A]	[1.4] [3.2] [3.8]	[1.4] [3.2] [3.3] [3.8] [4.A]	[3.3] [3.7] [3.8] [4.A] [5.2] [5.5]	[3.7] [3.8] [4.A] [5.2] [5.5]	[2.1] [2.3] [2.4] [2.7]	[2.1] [2.2] [2.7]	[2.2]	[3.7]		[3.3]
HIGH 100,000+	[1.2] [1.3] [3.7]	[3.1] [3.2] [4.A]			[3.2] [3.3] [3.7] [3.8] [4.A]	[1.2] [1.4] [3.2] [3.3] [3.8] [4.A]		[1.4] [3.2]		[1.4] [3.2]			[2.1] [2.2] [2.4] [2.7]	[2.1] [2.2] [2.7]	[2.2]	[3.7]		
ALL QUANTITIES	[1.1]	[1.1] [1.6] [3.4] [3.5]	[1.6]	[1.1] [1.6] [3.4] [3.5]	[1.1] [1.6] [3.4] [3.5] [5.5]	[1.1] [1.6] [3.4] [3.5]	[1.1] [3.4] [3.5]	[3.4] [3.5]			[1.1] [1.6] [3.4] [3.5]	[3.4] [3.5]				[5.5]	[1.6]	[1.6]

KEY TO MATRIX:

[1.1] SAND CASTING
[1.2] SHELL MOULDING
[1.3] GRAVITY DIE CASTING
[1.4] PRESSURE DIE CASTING
[1.5] CENTRIFUGAL CASTING
[1.6] INVESTMENT CASTING
[1.7] CERAMIC MOULD CASTING
[1.8] PLASTER MOULD CASTING

[2.1] INJECTION MOULDING
[2.2] COMPRESSION MOULDING
[2.3] VACUUM FORMING
[2.4] BLOW MOULDING
[2.5] ROTATIONAL MOULDING
[2.6] CONTACT MOULDING
[2.7] CONTINUOUS EXTRUSION (PLASTICS)

[3.1] CLOSED DIE FORGING/ UPSET FORGING
[3.2] COLD FORMING
[3.3] COLD HEADING
[3.4] SHEET METAL SHEARING
[3.5] SHEET METAL FORMING
[3.6] SPINNING
[3.7] POWDER METALLURGY
[3.8] CONTINUOUS EXTRUSION (METALS)

[4.A] AUTOMATIC MACHINING
[4.M] MANUAL MACHINING

(THE ABOVE HEADINGS COVER A BROAD RANGE OF MACHINING PROCESSES AND LEVELS OF CONTROL TECHNOLOGY. FOR MORE DETAIL, THE READER IS REFERRED TO THE INDIVIDUAL PROCESSES.)

[5.1] ELECTRICAL DISCHARGE MACHINING
[5.2] ELECTROCHEMICAL MACHINING
[5.3] ELECTRON BEAM MACHINING
[5.4] LASER BEAM MACHINING
[5.5] CHEMICAL MACHINING
[5.6] ULTRASONIC MACHINING

Figure 2.1 PRIMA selection matrix

To this end, a PRIMA selection matrix (see Figure 2.1) has been devised based on two basic variables:

- material type
- production quantity.

As mentioned previously there are many cost drivers in process selection, not least component size, geometry, tolerances, surface finish, capital equipment and labour costs. The justification for basing the matrix on material and production quantity is that they mix technological and economic issues of prime importance. The boundaries of economic production can be vague when so many factors are relevant, therefore, the matrix concentrates rather more on the use of materials.

By limiting itself in this way the matrix cannot be regarded as comprehensive and should not be taken as such. It represents the main common industrial practice but there will always be exceptions at this level of detail. It is not intended to represent a process selection methodology. The matrix is aimed at focusing attention on those PRIMAs that are most appropriate based on the important consideration of material and production quantity. It is the PRIMAs that do the business of guiding manufacturing process selection.

Note that conventional and non-traditional machining processes are often considered as secondary rather than primary manufacturing processes, although they can be applicable to both situations. The user should be aware of this when using the PRIMA selection matrix. Also, the conventional machining processes are grouped under just two headings in the matrix, manual and automatic machining. Reference should be made to the individual processes for more detail.

Fabrication and joining processes are not included in the selection matrix due to their unique application in assembly. Such processes can be used for all production quantities, including one-offs, and are used on many different types of material. Here, therefore, they are considered independent of the selection matrix and the reader is referred to the PRIMAs for detailed information on which to base selection.

2.3 Manufacturing process information maps (PRIMAs)

This section presents the PRIMAs for a number of important manufacturing processes. Each PRIMA is divided in to seven categories as listed and defined below, covering the characteristics and capabilities of the process:

- **Process description**: an explanation of the fundamentals of the process together with a diagrammatic representation of its operation.
- **Materials**: describes the materials currently suitable for the given process.
- **Process variations**: a description of any variations of the basic process and any special points related to those variations.
- **Economic considerations**: a list of several important points including: production rate, minimum production quantity, tooling costs, labour costs, lead times and any other points which may be of specific relevance to the process.
- **Typical applications**: a list of components and parts that have been successfully manufactured using the process.

- **Design aspects**: any points, opportunities or limitations that are relevant to the design of the part as well as standard information on minimum section, size range and general configuration.
- **Quality issues**: standard information includes a process capability chart, surface roughness and detail, as well as any information on possible faults, etc.

At the end of the book a list of source data and useful references for further reading is provided.

As mentioned previously, a key feature of the PRIMAs is the inclusion of process capability charts for most processes. Tolerances tend to be dependent on the overall dimension of the component characteristic and the relationship is specific and largely non-linear.

The charts have been developed to provide a simple means of understanding the influence of dimension on tolerance capability. The regions of the charts are divided by two contours. The region bounded by these two contours represents a spectrum of tolerance-dimension combinations where $C_{pk} \geq 1.33^*$ is achievable. Below this region, tolerance-dimension combinations are likely to require special control or secondary processing if $C_{pk} = 1.33$ is to be realized.

In the preparation of the charts it has been assumed that the geometry is well suited to the process and that all operational requirements are satisfied. Where the material under consideration is not mentioned on the charts, care should be taken. Any adverse affects due to this or geometrically driven component variation should be taken into consideration. For more information the reader is referred to references (2.2–2.4).

The information presented has been compiled from contacts in industry and from published work. As many as 20 different data sources have been used in the compilation of the individual process capability charts. Attempts have been made to standardize the data given as far as possible. Difficulties were faced in this connection since it was not always easy to obtain a consensus view.

$^*C_{pk}$ – process capability index. If the process characteristic is a normal distribution, C_{pk} can be related to a parts-per-million (ppm) defect rate. $C_{pk} = 1.33$ equates to a defect rate of 30 ppm at the nearest limit. At $C_{pk} = 1$, the defect rate equates to 1300 ppm.

1 Casting processes

1.1 Sand casting

Process description

- Moist bonded sand is packed around a pattern. The pattern is removed and molten metal poured into the cavity. Risers supply necessary molten material during solidification. The mould is broken to remove the part.

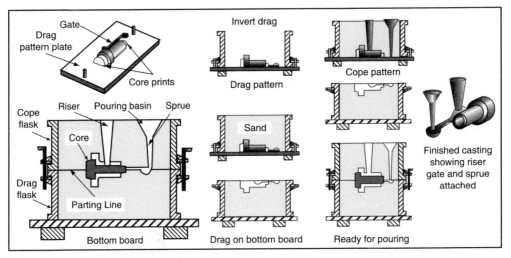

Materials

- Most metals. Some difficulty encountered in casting: lead, tin and zinc alloys, also refractory alloys, beryllium, titanium and zirconia alloys.

Process variations

- Green sand casting: the most common and the cheapest. Associated problems are that the mould has low strength and high moisture content.
- Dry sand: core boxes are used instead of patterns. Expensive and time consuming.
- Skin-dried sand: the mould is dried to a certain depth. Used in the casting of steels.
- Patterns: one piece solid patterns are cheapest to make; split patterns for moderate quantities; match plate patterns for high volume production.
- Wooden patterns: low volume production only.
- Metal patterns: for medium to high volume production.
- Hard plastics are increasingly being used.

Economic considerations

- Production rates of 1–60 pieces/hour, but dependent on size.
- Lead time ranges from days to several weeks depending on complexity and size of casting.

- Material utilization is low to moderate – 20–50% of material lost in runners and risers.
- Both mould material and runners and risers may be recycled.
- Patterns are easy to make and set, and are reusable.
- Pattern material dependent on the number of castings required.
- Easy to change design during production.
- Economical for low production runs. Can be used for one-offs.
- Tooling costs are low.
- Equipment costs are low.
- Direct labour costs are moderate to high. Can be labour intensive.
- Finishing costs can be high. Cleaning and fettling are important before secondary processing.

Typical applications

- Engine blocks.
- Manifolds.
- Machine tool bases.
- Pump housings.
- Cylinder heads.

Design aspects

- High degree of shape complexity possible. Limited only by the pattern.
- Loose piece patterns can be used for holes and protrusions.
- All intersecting surfaces must be filleted: prevents shrinkage cracks and eliminates stress concentrations.
- Design of gating system for delivery of molten metal into mould cavity important.
- Placing of parting line important, i.e. avoid placement across critical dimensions.
- Bosses, undercuts and inserts are all possible at low added cost.
- Machining allowances are usually in the range 1.5–6 mm.
- Draft angle ranges from 1 to 5°.
- Minimum section typically 3 mm for light alloys and 6 mm for ferrous alloys.
- Sizes range from 20 g to 400 t in weight.

Quality issues

- Moulding sand must be carefully conditioned and controlled.
- Most casting defects can be traced to and rectified by sand content.
- Casting shrinkage and distortion during cooling governed by shape, especially when one dimension is much larger than the other two.
- Extensive flat surfaces are prone to sand expansion defects.
- Inspection of castings is important.
- High porosity and inclusion levels are common in castings.
- Defects in castings may be filled with weld material.
- Castings generally have rough grainy surfaces.
- Material strength is inherently poor.

- Castings have good bearing and damping properties.
- If production volumes warrant the cost of a die, close tolerances may be achieved.
- Surface detail fair to moderate.
- Surface roughness is a function of the materials used in making the mould and is in the range from 3.2 to 50 μm *Ra*.
- Not suitable for close specification of tolerances without secondary processing.
- Process capability charts showing the achievable dimensional tolerances using various materials are given below. Allowances of ±0.5 to ±2 mm should be added for dimensions across the parting line.

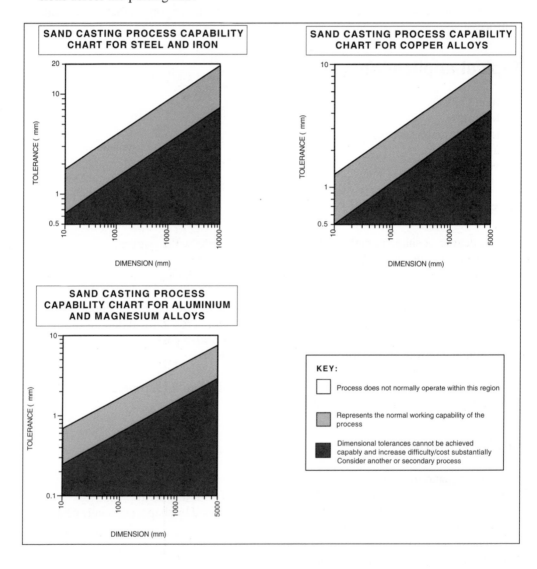

1.2 Shell moulding

Process description

- A heated metal pattern is placed over a box of resin coated sand. The box is inverted for a fixed time curing the sand. The box is re-inverted and the excess sand falls out. The shell is then removed from the pattern and joined with the other half (previously made). They are supported in a flask by an inert material ready for casting.

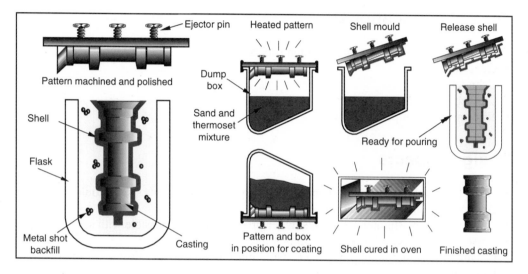

Materials

- Most metals, except: lead, zinc, magnesium and titanium alloys, also beryllium, refractory and zirconia alloys.

Process variations

- Moulds produced from other casting processes may be joined with shell moulds.
- Patterns are generally made of iron or steel which give good dimensional accuracy; aluminium may be used for low volume production.
- Other pattern materials used are plaster, and graphite.

Economic considerations

- Production rates of 5–200 pieces/hour, but dependent on size.
- Lead time varies from several days to weeks depending on complexity and size.
- Material utilization is high; little scrap generated.
- Potential for automation high.
- With use of gating systems several castings in a single mould are possible.

- Resin binders cost more but only 5% as much sand is used as compared to sand casting.
- Difficult to change design during production.
- More suited to moderate to high volume production. Production volumes of 100–500 pieces may be economical.
- Considered best of the low-cost casting methods for large quantities.
- Tooling costs are low to moderate.
- Equipment costs are moderate to high.
- Labour costs are low to moderate.
- Low finishing costs. Often no finishing required.

Typical applications

- Small mechanical parts requiring high precision.
- Gear housings.
- Cylinder heads.
- Connecting rods.
- Transmission components.

Design aspects

- Good for moulding complex shapes, especially when using composite moulds.
- Great variations in cross-section possible.
- Sharper corners, thinner sections, smaller projections than possible with sand casting.
- Bosses, undercuts and inserts are all possible.
- Placing of parting line important, i.e. avoid placement across critical dimensions.
- Draft angle ranges from 0.1° to 3°.
- Maximum section = 50 mm.
- Minimum section = 1.5 mm.
- Sizes range from 10 g to 150 kg in weight. Better for small parts (<20 kg).

Quality issues

- Blowing sand onto the pattern makes depositing more uniform, especially good for intricate forms.
- Few castings are scrapped due to blowholes or pockets (gases are able to escape through thin shells).
- Composite cores may include chills and cores to control solidification rate in critical areas.
- Moderate porosity and inclusions.
- Mechanical properties are better than sand casting.
- Uniform grain structure.
- Surface detail good.
- Surface roughnesses in the range 0.8–12.5 µm *Ra* can be achieved.
- Process capability charts showing the achievable dimensional tolerances using various materials are given on the next page. Allowances of ±0.25 to ±0.5 mm should be added for dimensions across the parting line.

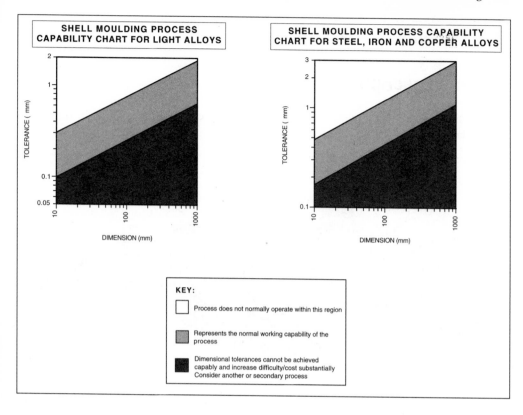

SHELL MOULDING PROCESS CAPABILITY CHART FOR LIGHT ALLOYS

TOLERANCE (mm)

DIMENSION (mm)

SHELL MOULDING PROCESS CAPABILITY CHART FOR STEEL, IRON AND COPPER ALLOYS

TOLERANCE (mm)

DIMENSION (mm)

KEY:

Process does not normally operate within this region

Represents the normal working capability of the process

Dimensional tolerances cannot be achieved capably and increase difficulty/cost substantially Consider another or secondary process

1.3 Gravity die casting

Process description

- Molten metal is poured under gravity into a pre-heated metallic, graphite or refractory die where it solidifies. The die is then opened and the casting ejected.

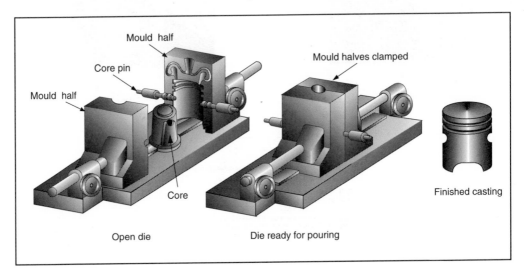

Materials

- Usually non-ferrous metals, for example: copper, aluminium, magnesium, but sometimes iron, lead, nickel, tin and zinc alloys. Carbon steel can be cast with graphite dies.

Process variations

- Low pressure die casting: uses low pressure air to force the molten metal into the die cavity. Less popular than gravity and tends to be used purely for the production of car wheels.

Economic considerations

- Production rates of 5–100 pieces/hour common, but dependent on size.
- Lead times can be many weeks.
- Material utilization is high.
- There is little scrap generated.
- If accuracy and surface finish is not an issue, can use sand cores instead of metallic or graphite for greater economy.
- Production volumes of 500–1000 may be viable.
- Suited to high volume production.

- Tooling costs are moderate.
- Equipment costs are moderate.
- Labour costs are low to moderate.
- Finishing costs are low to moderate.

Typical applications

- Cylinder heads.
- Connecting rods.
- Pistons.
- Gear and die blanks.

Design aspects

- Shape complexity limited by that obtained in die halves.
- Undercuts are possible with large added cost.
- Inserts are possible with small added cost.
- Machining allowances are usually in the range from 0.8 to 1.5 mm.
- Placing of parting line important, i.e. avoid placement across critical dimensions.
- Draft angle ranges from 0.1° to 3°.
- Maximum section = 50 mm.
- Minimum section = 2 mm.
- Sizes range from 100 g to 300 kg in weight. Commonly used for castings <5 kg.

Quality issues

- Little porosity and inclusions.
- Redressing of the dies may be required after several thousand castings.
- Collapsible cores improve extraction difficulties on cooling.
- 'Chilling' effect of cold metallic dies on the surface of the solidifying metals needs to be controlled by pre-heating at correct temperature.
- Large castings sometimes require that the die is tilted as molten metal is being poured in to reduce turbulence.
- Mechanical properties are fair to good.
- Surface detail good.
- Surface roughnesses in the range 0.8 to 6.3 µm *Ra* can be achieved.
- Process capability charts showing the achievable dimensional tolerances using various materials are given on the next page. Allowances of ±0.25 to ±0.75 mm should be added for dimensions across the parting line.

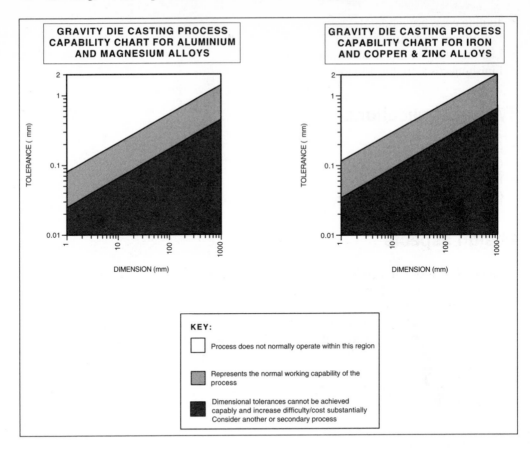

1.4 Pressure die casting

Process description

- Molten metal is inserted into a metallic mould under pressure where it solidifies. The die is then opened and the casting ejected.

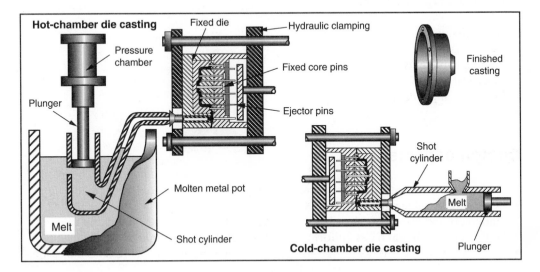

Materials

- Limited to non-ferrous metals, i.e. zinc, aluminium, magnesium, lead, tin and copper alloys.
- Zinc and aluminium alloys tend to be the most popular.
- High temperature metals, e.g. copper alloys, reduce die life.
- Iron based materials for casting are under development.

Process variations

- Cold-chamber die casting is used for high melting temperature metals.
- Hot-chamber die casting is used for low melting temperature metals due to erosive nature of molten metal. Can be either plunger or goose-neck type.

Economic considerations

- Rapid production rates possible, up to 200 pieces/hour.
- Lead time could run into months.
- Material utilization is high.
- Gates, sprues, etc., can be re-melted.
- High initial die costs due to high complexity and difficulty to process.

- Production quantities of ≥ 10,000 are economical.
- Tooling costs are high.
- Equipment costs are high.
- Direct labour costs are low to moderate.
- Finishing costs are low. Little more than trimming operations required to remove flash, etc.

Typical applications

- Transmission cases.
- Engine parts.
- Pump components.
- Electrical boxes.
- Domestic appliances.
- Toy parts.

Design aspects

- Shape complexity can be high. Limited by design of movable cores.
- Bosses are possible with added costs.
- Undercuts and inserts are possible with added costs and reduced production rates.
- Wall thickness should be as uniform as possible; transitions should be gradual.
- Sharp corners, or corners without proper radii should be avoided. (Pressure die casting permits smaller radii because metal flow is aided.)
- Placing of parting line important, i.e. avoid placement across critical dimensions.
- Holes perpendicular to the parting line can be cast.
- Casting holes for subsequent tapping is generally more economical than drilling.
- Machining allowance is normally in the range from 0.25 to 0.8 mm.
- Draft angle ranges from 0.5 to 3°.
- Maximum section = 12 mm.
- Minimum section ranges from 0.4 to 1.5 mm depending on material used.
- Sizes range from 10 g to 50 kg. Castings up to 100 kg have been made in zinc. Copper, tin and lead castings are normally less than 5 kg.

Quality issues

- Very low porosity.
- Particularly suited where casting requires high mechanical properties or absence of creep.
- The high melting temperature of some metals can cause significant processing difficulties and die wear.
- Difficulty is experienced in obtaining sound castings in the larger capacities due to gas entrapment.
- Close control of temperature, pressure and cooling times important in obtaining consistent quality castings.
- Mechanical properties are good.

- Surface detail excellent.
- Surface roughnesses in the range 0.4 to 3.2 µm *Ra* can be achieved.
- Process capability charts showing the achievable dimensional tolerances using various materials are given below. Allowances of ±0.05 to ±0.35 mm should be added for dimensions across the parting line.

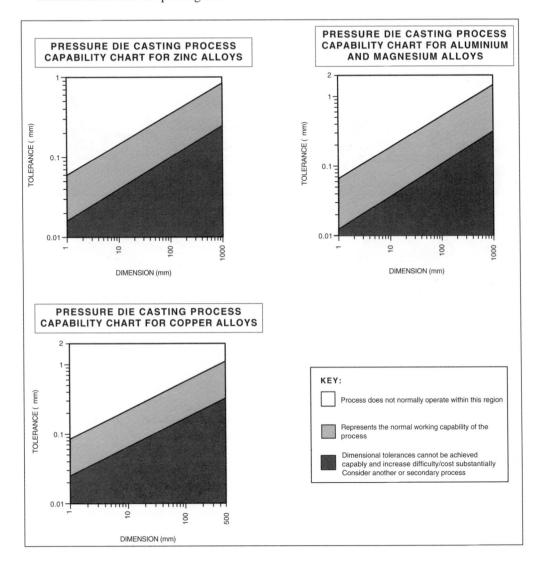

1.5 Centrifugal casting

Process description

- Molten metal is poured into a rotating mould. The axis of rotation is usually horizontal, but may be vertical for short workpieces.

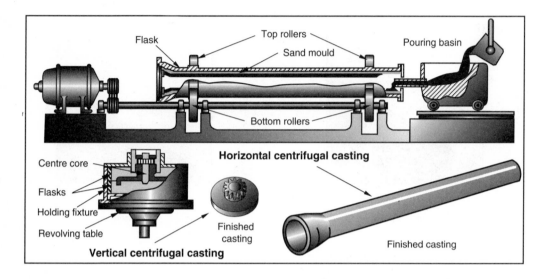

Materials

- Most metals suitable for static casting are suitable for centrifugal casting: steels, iron, copper, aluminium and nickel alloys.
- Also, glass, plastics and ceramics (metal moulds sprayed with a refractory material).

Process variations

- Semi-centrifugal casting: used to cast parts with radial symmetry.
- Centrifuging: mould cavities of any shape are placed a certain distance from the axis of rotation. Molten metal is poured from the centre and forced into the mould by centrifugal forces. Properties of castings vary by distance from the axis of rotation.

Economic considerations

- Production rates of up to 50 pieces/hour possible, but dependent on size.
- Lead time may be several weeks.
- Material utilization high (90–100%) – no runners or risers.
- Economic when the mechanical properties of thick walled tubes are important and high alloy grades of steel are required.

- In large quantities production of other than circular external shapes becomes more economical.
- Mild steel tubes made by this method with small diameters are not competitive with welded or rolled tubes.
- Selection of mould type (permanent or sand) is determined by shape of casting, quality and number to be produced.
- Production volumes are low. Can be used for one-offs.
- Tooling costs are moderate.
- Equipment costs are moderate to high.
- Direct labour costs are low to moderate.
- Finishing costs are low to moderate. Normally, machining of internal dimension necessary.

Typical applications

- Pipes.
- Brake drums.
- Pulley wheels.
- Gun barrels.
- Bushes and gears.
- Engine-cylinder liners.
- Pressure vessels.

Design aspects

- Shape complexity limited by nature of process.
- Circular bore remains in the finished part.
- Dual metal tubes that combine the properties of two metals in one application are possible.
- Inserts and bosses are possible, but undercuts are not.
- Placing of parting line important, i.e. avoid placement across critical dimensions.
- Machining allowances range from 1.5 to 6 mm.
- Draft angle approximately 1°.
- Maximum section thickness approximately 100 mm.
- Minimum section ranges from 2 to 8 mm, depending on material cast.
- Sizes range from $\varnothing25$ mm to $\varnothing1.8$ m.

Quality issues

- Due to density differences in the molten material, dross, impurities and pieces of the refractory lining tend to collect on the inner surface of the casting. This may be machined away.
- Tubular castings have higher structural strengths and more distinct cast impressions than gravity die casting or sand cast produced parts.
- Castings are free of shrinkage due to one-directional cooling.

- The properties of dense castings are comparable with forgings.
- Low porosity.
- Good mechanical properties and fine grain structure.
- Surface detail fair to good.
- Surface roughnesses in the range 1.6 to 12.5 mm *Ra* can be achieved.
- A process capability chart showing the achievable dimensional tolerances is given below. Allowances of approximately ±0.25 to ±0.75 mm should be added for dimensions across the parting line. Note, that the chart applies to outside dimensions only. Internal dimensions are approximately 50% greater.

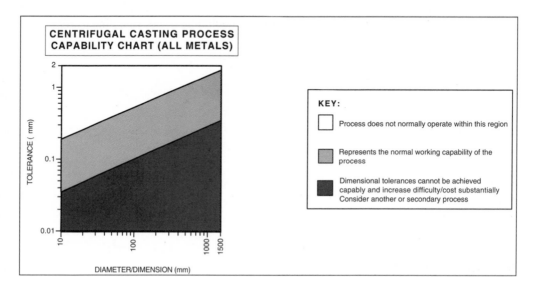

1.6 Investment casting

Process description

- A mould is used to generate a wax pattern of the shape required. A ceramic slurry is cast around the wax pattern, the wax melted out and the metal cast in the ceramic mould. The mould is then destroyed to remove the casting. Process often known as the 'Lost Wax' process.

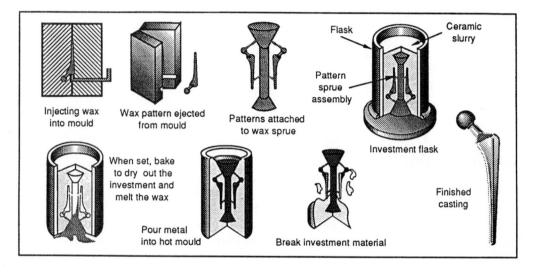

Injecting wax into mould

Wax pattern ejected from mould

Patterns attached to wax sprue

Flask

Pattern sprue assembly

Ceramic slurry

Investment flask

When set, bake to dry out the investment and melt the wax

Pour metal into hot mould

Break investment material

Finished casting

Materials

- All metals, including precious, reactive and radioactive alloys (cast in vacuum).

Process variations

- Use of thermoplastic resin instead of wax.

Economic considerations

- Production rates of up to 1000 pieces/hour, depending on size.
- Lead times are usually several weeks, but can be shorter.
- Best suited to metals having high melting temperatures, and/or which are difficult to machine or which have a high cost.
- Material utilization is high.
- Pattern costs can be high for low quantities.
- Ceramic and wax cores allow complex internal configurations to be produced, but increase the cost significantly.
- Wax or plastic patterns can be injection moulded for high production runs.

- A 'tree' of wax patterns enables many small castings to be handled together.
- Suitable for small batches (10–1000) and high volume production.
- Tooling costs moderate, but dependent on complexity.
- Equipment costs are low to moderate (high when processing reactive materials).
- Labour costs are high. Can be labour intensive as many hand operations required.
- Low finishing costs. Gates and feeders are removed by machining and the piece may be cleaned by sand/bead blasting.

Typical applications

- Turbine blades.
- Machine tool parts.
- Aeroengine components.
- Pump casings.
- Automotive engine components.
- Figurines.
- Jewellery.

Design aspects

- Very complex castings with unusual internal configurations possible.
- Wax pattern must be easily removable from its mould.
- Complex shapes may be assembled from several simpler shapes.
- Practical way of producing threads in hard to machine materials, or where thread design is unusual.
- Uniform sections are preferred. Abrupt changes should be gradually blended in or designed out.
- Fillets should be as generous as possible.
- Holes, both blind and through are possible. Length to diameter ratio for blind holes is typically 4:1.
- Bosses and undercuts are possible with added cost.
- Inserts are not possible.
- Machining allowance usually between 0.3 and 2 mm, depending on size.
- Draft angle usually zero, but 0.5 to 1° desirable on long extended surfaces, or if mould cavity is deep.
- Minimum section ranges from 0.25 to 1 mm, depending on material cast.
- Maximum section is approximately 75 mm.
- Sizes range from 0.5 g to 100 kg in weight, but best for parts <5 kg.

Quality issues

- Moderate porosity.
- High strength castings are produced.
- Grain growth more pronounced in longer sections which may limit the toughness and fatigue life of the part.
- Good to excellent surface detail possible.

- Surface roughness in the range 0.4 to 6.3 µm *Ra* can be achieved.
- A process capability chart showing the achievable dimensional tolerances is given below.
- No parting line on casting.

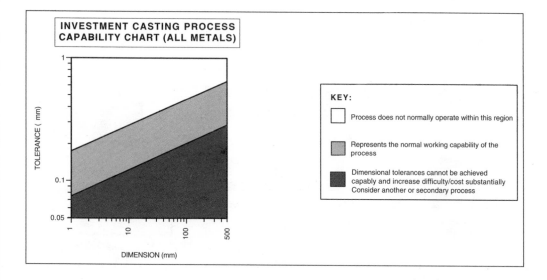

INVESTMENT CASTING PROCESS CAPABILITY CHART (ALL METALS)

TOLERANCE (mm)

DIMENSION (mm)

KEY:

Process does not normally operate within this region

Represents the normal working capability of the process

Dimensional tolerances cannot be achieved capably and increase difficulty/cost substantially Consider another or secondary process

1.7 Ceramic mould casting

Process description

- A precision metal pattern generates the mould which is made of a ceramic slurry. The mould is dried and baked. The molten metal is then poured into the mould and allowed to solidify. The mould is broken to remove the part.

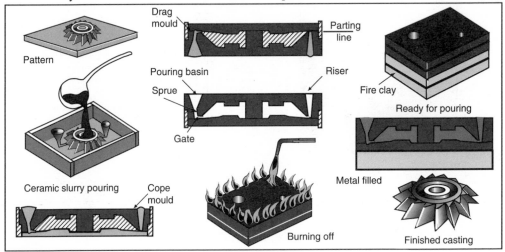

Materials

- All metals, but to lesser degree aluminium, magnesium, zinc, tin and copper alloys.

Process variations

- Variations on the composition of the ceramic slurry and curing mechanisms exist.

Economic considerations

- Production rates of up to 10 pieces/hour normal.
- Lead times can be several days.
- Material utilization is high.
- Low scrap losses.
- Best suited to metals having high melting temperatures and/or that are difficult to machine.
- Can be combined with investment casting to produce parts with increased complexity with reduced cost.
- Suitable for small batches and medium volume production.
- Can be used for one-offs.
- Tooling costs are low.
- Equipment costs are moderate.
- Direct labour costs are moderate to high.
- Finishing costs are low. Usually no machining is required.

Typical applications

- All types of dies and moulds for other casting and forming processes.
- Cutting tool bodies.
- Components for food handling machining.
- Pump impellers.
- Aerospace and atomic reactor components.

Design aspects

- High complexity possible – almost any shape possible.
- Use of cores increase complexity obtainable.
- Inserts, bosses and undercuts are possible with little added cost.
- Placing of parting line important, i.e. avoid placement across critical dimensions.
- Where machining is required, allowances of up to 0.6 mm should be observed.
- Draft angle usually zero, but 0.1–1° preferred.
- Minimum section ranges from 0.6 to 1.2 mm, depending on material used.
- Sizes range from 100 g to 3 t in weight.

Quality issues

- Low porosity.
- Mechanical properties are good.
- Good surface detail possible.
- Surface roughnesses in the range from 0.8 to 6.3 μm *Ra* can be achieved.
- A process capability chart showing the achievable dimensional tolerances is given below. An allowance of ±0.25 mm should be added for dimensions across the parting line.
- Parting lines are sometimes pronounced on finished casting.

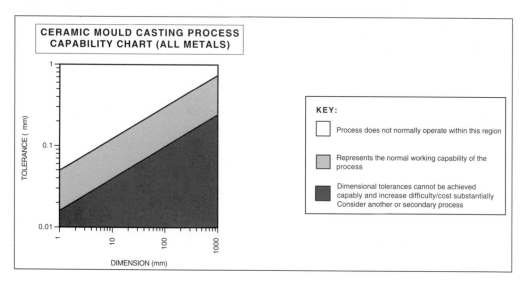

1.8   Plaster mould casting

Process description

- A precision metal pattern (usually brass) generates the two-part mould which is made of a gypsum slurry material. The mould is removed from the pattern and baked to remove the moisture. The molten metal is poured into the mould and allowed to cool. The mould is broken to remove the part.

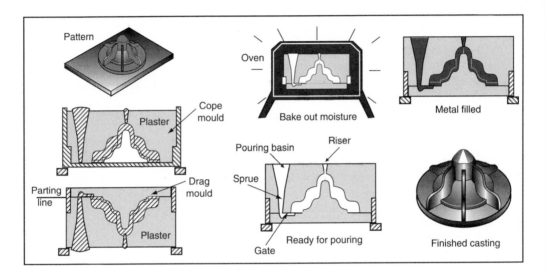

Materials

- Limited to low melting temperature metals, i.e. aluminium, copper, zinc and magnesium alloys due to degradation of the plaster mould at elevated temperatures.
- Tin and lead alloys are sometimes processed.

Process variations

- Patterns can be made from: metal, plaster, wood or thermosetting plastic. Wood has a limited life due to water absorption from the plaster slurry.
- Composition of plaster slurry varies. Additives are sometimes used to control mould expansion and fibres added to improve mould strength.

Economic considerations

- Production rates of up to 10 pieces/hour normal.
- Lead times can be several days to weeks.
- Material utilization is high.

- Low scrap losses. Waste is recycled.
- Mould destroyed in removing casting.
- Easy to change design during production.
- Suitable for small batches (10–100) and medium volume production.
- Tooling costs are low to moderate.
- Equipment costs are moderate.
- Direct labour costs are high. Some skilled operations necessary.
- Finishing costs are low. Little finishing required except grinding for gate removal.

Typical applications

- Pump impellers.
- Waveguide components (for use in microwave applications).
- Lock components.
- Gears.
- Valve parts.
- Moulds for plastic and rubber processing, i.e. tyre moulds.

Design aspects

- Moderate to high complexity possible.
- Possible to make mould from several pieces.
- Deep holes are not recommended.
- Sharp corners and features can be cast easily.
- Inserts, bosses and undercuts are possible with little added cost.
- Placing of parting line important, i.e. avoid placement across critical dimensions.
- Where machining is required, allowances of up to 0.8 mm should be observed.
- Draft angles from 0.5 to 1° preferred, but can be zero.
- Minimum section ranges from 0.8 to 1.8 mm, depending on material used.
- Sizes range from 25 g to 50 kg in weight. However, castings up to 1000 kg have been made.

Quality issues

- Little or no distortion on thin sections.
- Plaster mould has low permeability and can create gas evolution problems.
- Moderate to high porosity obtained.
- Mechanical properties are fair.
- Surface detail good.
- Surface roughness in the range from 0.8 to 3.2 mm *Ra* can be achieved.
- A process capability chart showing the achievable dimensional tolerances is given on the next page. An allowance of approximately ±0.25 mm should be added for dimensions across the parting line.

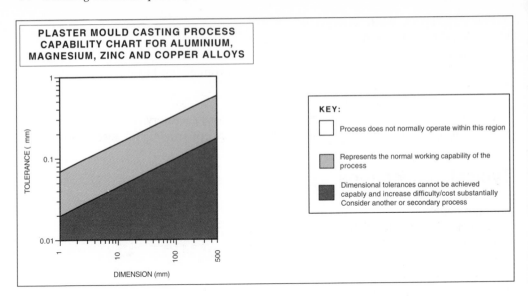

2 Plastic and composite processing

2.1   Injection moulding

Process description

- Granules of unpolymerized material are heated and then forced, under pressure into the die cavity. Components produced have characteristic sprues left on surface.

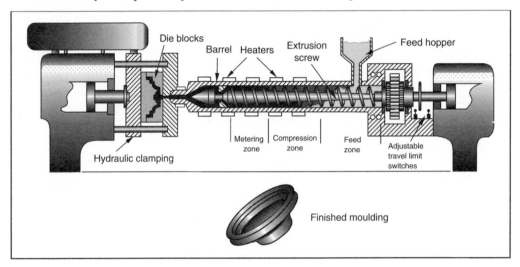

Materials

- Mostly thermoplastics, but thermosets, composites and elastomers can also be processed.

Process variations

- Reaction injection moulding: two reactive fluids are forced under pressure into the mould producing a thermoset part (chemical reaction is irreversible).

Economic considerations

- Production rates are high, cycle times of 10–60 seconds typical.
- Thermoset parts usually have a longer cycle time.
- Lead times can be several weeks due to manufacturing of complex dies.
- Material utilization is good. Scrap generated in sprues and risers.
- If material permits, gates and runners can be reused resulting in low material loss.
- Flexibility limited by dedicated dies, die changeover and machine set-up times.
- Economical for high production runs – typically >10,000.
- Tooling costs are high. Dies are usually made from tool steel.
- Equipment costs are moderate to high.
- Direct labour costs are low.
- Finishing costs are low – little trimming required.

Typical applications

- High precision, complex plastic components.
- Electrical parts.
- Fittings.
- Containers.
- Bottle tops.
- Housings.
- Tool handles.

Design aspects

- Very complex shapes and intricate detail possible.
- Pockets, holes, bosses and minor re-entrant features common.
- Radii should be as generous as possible.
- Uniform section thickness should be maintained.
- Marked section changes should be tapered sufficiently.
- Living hinges and snap features allow part consolidation.
- Thread forms also possible.
- Placing of parting line important, i.e. avoid placement across critical dimensions.
- Inserts may be moulded in (e.g. metallic inserts for electrical conduction).
- The clamping force required is proportional to the projected area of the moulded part.
- Draft angle ranges from less than 1–3° typically, depending on section depth.
- Maximum section, typically = 13 mm.
- Minimum section = 0.4 mm for thermoplastics, 1 mm for thermosets.
- Sizes range from 10 g to 25 kg in weight for thermoplastics, 6 kg maximum for thermosets.

Quality issues

- Thick sections can be problematic.
- Care must be taken in the design of the running and gating system, where multiple cavities are used to ensure complete die fill.
- Unsuitable for the production of narrow necked containers.
- Control of temperature (material and mould) is critical, also injection pressure/speed, condition of resin, dwell and cooling times.
- Adequate clamping force is necessary to prevent the mould from flashing.
- Thermoplastic moulded parts usually require no de-flashing: thermoset parts often require this operation.
- Excellent surface detail obtainable.
- Surface roughness is a function of the die condition. Typically, 0.2–0.8 μm *Ra* is obtainable.
- Process capability charts showing the achievable dimensional tolerances using various materials (see key) are given on the next page. Allowances of approximately ±0.1 mm should be added for dimensions across the parting line. Note that charts 1–3 are to be used for components which have a major dimension greater than 50 mm and typically large production volumes. The chart entitled 'light engineering' is used typically for components with a major dimension less than 150 mm and for small production volumes.

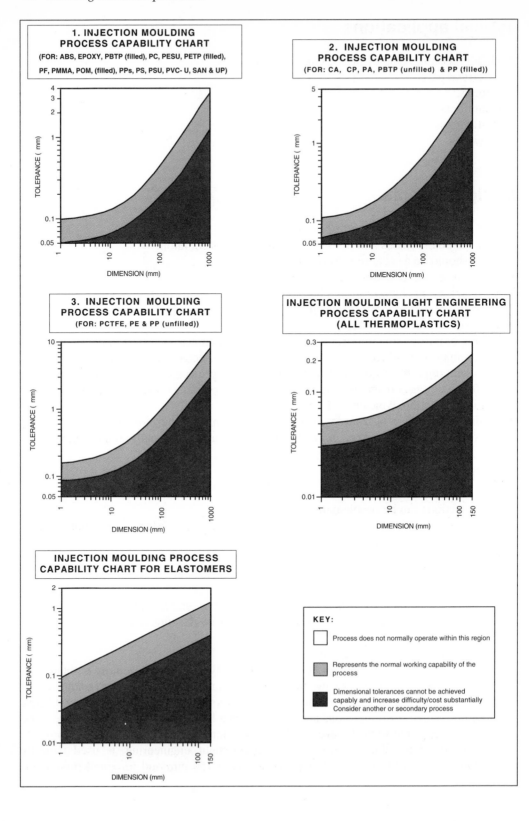

Material key for plastic moulding processes

ABS	Acrylonitrile butadiene styrene
CA	Cellulose acetate
CP	Cellulose propionate
PF	Phenolic
PA	Polyamide
PBTP	Polybutylene terephthalate
PC	Polycarbonate
PCTFE	Polychlorotrifluoroethylene
PE	Polyethylene
PESU	Polyethersulphone
PETP	Polyethyleneterephthalate
PMMA	Polymethylmethacrylate
POM	Polyoxymethylene
PPS	Polyphenylene sulphide
PP	Polypropylene
PS	Polystyrene
PSU	Polysulphone
PVC-U	Polyvinylchloride – unplasticized
SAN	Styrene acrylonitrile
UP	Polyester
SMC	Sheet moulding compounds
BMC	Bulk moulding compounds.

2.2 Compression moulding

Process description

- An appropriate quantity of the raw, unpolymerized plastic is introduced into a heated mould which is subsequently closed under pressure, forcing the material into all areas of the cavity as it melts. Similar to closed die forging of metals.

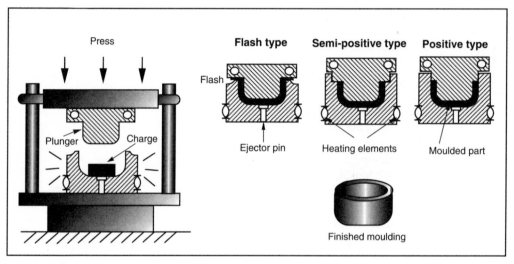

Materials

- Mainly thermosets, but also some composites, elastomers and thermoplastics.

Process variations

- Flash-type: shallow parts; more material lost.
- Semi-positive (partly positive, partly flash): used for closer tolerances work and when the design involves marked changes in section thickness.
- Positive: high density parts involving composite sheet and bulk moulding compounds or impact-thermosetting materials.
- Cold-moulding: powder or filler (often refractory) is mixed with a binder, compressed in a cold die and cured in an oven.

Economic considerations

- Production cycle times from 20 to 600 seconds typically.
- Cycle time is restricted by material handling; each cavity must be loaded individually.
- The greater the thickness of the part, the longer the curing time.
- Multiple cavity moulds increase production rate.
- Mould maintenance is minimal.

- Time required for polymerization (curing) depends mainly on the largest cross-section of the product and the type of moulding compound.
- Lead times may be several weeks according to die complexity.
- Material utilization is high (no sprues or runners).
- Flexibility is low. Differences in shrinkage properties reduces the capability to change from one material to another.
- Production volumes are typically >1000, but can be as low as 100 for large parts.
- Tooling costs are generally high.
- Equipment costs are moderate to high.
- Direct labour and finishing costs are generally low. Flash removal required.

Typical applications

- Dishes.
- Handles.
- Container caps.
- Electrical components and fittings.

Design aspects

- Shape complexity is limited to relatively simple forms. Moulding in one plane only.
- Holes, protrusions, pockets and minor re-entrant features are possible.
- Inserts can be moulded in to achieve special properties.
- Thin-walled parts with minimum warping and dimensional deviation may be moulded.
- When moulding materials with reinforcing fibres, fibre directionality is maintained enabling high strength to be achieved.
- Placing of parting line important, i.e. avoid placement across critical dimensions.
- A draft angle of greater than 1° required.
- Maximum section, typically = 25 mm.
- Minimum section = 0.25 mm.
- Sizes range from several gram to 15 kg in weight.

Quality issues

- Variation in polymer charge results in variation of part thickness.
- Air entrapment possible.
- Internal stresses are minimal.
- Dimensions in the direction of the mould opening and the product density will tend to vary more than those perpendicular to the mould opening.
- Flash moulds do not require that the quantity of material is controlled.
- Tumbling may be required as finishing process because of flash.
- Surface roughness is a function of the die condition. Typically, 0.2–0.8 μm *Ra* is obtained.
- Process capability charts showing the achievable dimensional tolerances using various materials are given on the next page. Allowances of approximately ±0.1 mm should be added for dimensions across the parting line.

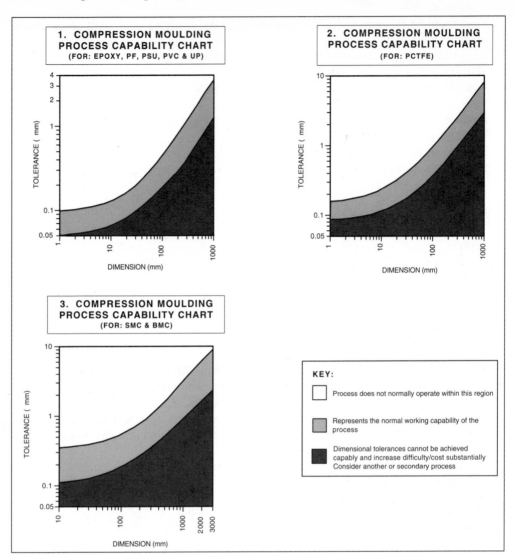

2.3 Vacuum forming

Process description

- A plastic sheet is softened by heating elements and pulled under vacuum on to the surface form of a cold mould and allowed to cool. The part is then removed.

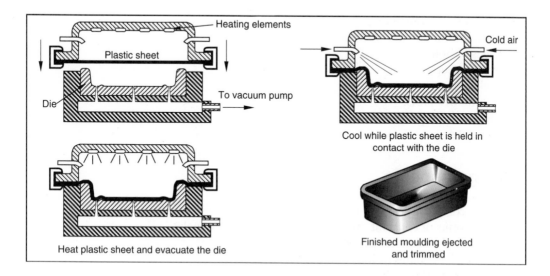

Heating elements

Plastic sheet

Die

To vacuum pump

Heat plastic sheet and evacuate the die

Cold air

Cool while plastic sheet is held in contact with the die

Finished moulding ejected and trimmed

Materials

- Most thermoplastics.
- The material to be processed should exhibit high uniform elongation.

Process variations

- Moulds are usually made of cast aluminium or aluminium-filled epoxy.
- Top and bottom heating elements.
- Top heating elements only.

Economic considerations

- Process cycle times range from 10 to 60 seconds.
- Lead times of a few days typical, but can be weeks.
- Material utilization is moderate to low: unformed parts of the sheet are lost and cannot be directly recycled.
- Multiple moulds may be used.

- Set-up times and change-over times are low.
- Production volume trends vary from small batches (10) to high volume, >1000.
- Tooling costs are low to moderate, depending on complexity.
- Equipment costs are low to moderate, but can be high if automated.
- Labour costs are low to moderate.
- Finishing costs are low.

Typical applications

- Open plastic containers.
- Panels for non-heavy fixtures.
- Pages of braille text.
- Vending cups.
- Packaging.
- Automotive parts.
- Electronic enclosures.
- Bath tubs.

Design aspects

- Shape complexity limited to mouldings in one plane.
- Open forms of constant thickness without re-entrant angles.
- Bosses and inserts not possible.
- Parts with openings or holes cannot be formed.
- Corner radii should be large compared to thickness of material.
- Draft angles of 1° or greater recommended.
- Maximum section = 3 mm.
- Minimum section = 0.05–0.5 mm, depending on material used.
- Sizes range from 25 mm^2 to 7.5 m × 2.5 m in area.

Quality issues

- Control of temperature, clamping force and vacuum pressure are important if variability is to be minimized.
- If multiple moulds are used it is necessary that there is sufficient distance between cavities to avoid flow interference.
- Excessive thinning can occur, particularly at sharp corners.
- Surface detail fair.
- Surface finish is good and is related to the condition of mould surface.
- Achievable tolerances range from ±0.25 to ±2 mm, and are largely mould dependent.
- No parting lines.

2.4   Blow moulding

Process description

- A hot hollow tube of plastic (parison) is extruded or injected downwards and then caught between two halves of a shaped mould which closes the top and bottom of the tube. Hot air is blown into the parison, expanding it until it uniformly contacts the inside contours of the cold mould. The part is allowed to cool and is then ejected.

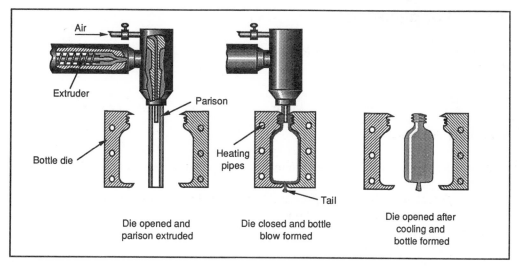

Die opened and parison extruded

Die closed and bottle blow formed

Die opened after cooling and bottle formed

Materials

- Most thermoplastics. PETP most commonly used.

Process variations

- Injection blow moulding: small parts with intricate neck detail.
- Extrusion blow moulding: more applicable to asymmetrical parts, integrated handles possible.
- Multiple parisons: this requires close control since uneven parisons produce waste.
- Parisonless blowing: similar to dip-coating followed by expansion into the mould.
- Stretch blow moulding: the simultaneous axial and radial expansion of a parison, yielding a biaxially orientated container.
- Pressure moulding with an inert gas (compare with vacuum forming).

Economic considerations

- Production rates between 100–2500 pieces/hour, depending on size.
- Lead times are a few days.

- Integration with extrusion process to produce parison provides continuous operation.
- There is generally little material waste, but can be high with some geometries.
- Flexibility is limited since moulds are dedicated.
- Set-up times and change-over times are relatively short.
- Production volumes of up to 10,000,000, but also suitable for quantities as low as 1000.
- Tooling costs are moderate to high.
- Equipment costs are moderate to high.
- Direct labour costs are low: one operator can mange several machines.
- Finishing cots are low: trimming only.

Typical applications

- Hollow plastic parts with relatively thin walls.
- Bottles.
- Bumpers.
- Ducting.

Design aspects

- Complexity limited to hollow, well rounded, thin walled parts with low degree of asymmetry.
- Asymmetrical mouldings, e.g. offset necks are possible with movable blowing spigots.
- Threads, inserts and undercuts all possible.
- Corner radii should be as generous as possible.
- Placing of parting line important, i.e. avoid placement across critical dimensions.
- Holes cannot be moulded.
- Draft angles not required.
- Maximum section = 6 mm. Thick sections may need cooling aids (carbon dioxide or nitrogen).
- Minimum section = 0.25 mm.
- Sizes range from 12 mm in length to volumes up to 3 m^3.

Quality issues

- Poor control of wall thickness, typically ±50% of nominal.
- Creep and chemical stability of product are important considerations.
- Residual stresses, e.g. non-uniform deformation, may relax in time causing distortion of the part.
- Good surface detail and finish possible.
- The higher the pressure the better the surface finish of the product.
- A process capability chart showing the achievable dimensional tolerances is given on the next page. Allowances of approximately ±0.1 mm should be added for dimensions across the parting line.

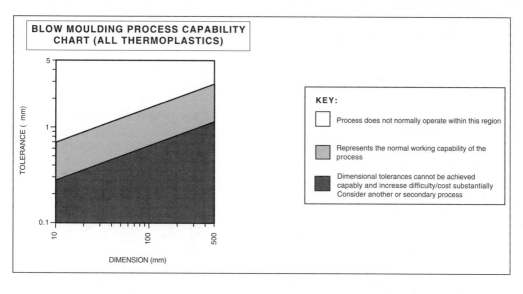

BLOW MOULDING PROCESS CAPABILITY
CHART (ALL THERMOPLASTICS)

KEY:

Process does not normally operate within this region

Represents the normal working capability of the process

Dimensional tolerances cannot be achieved capably and increase difficulty/cost substantially Consider another or secondary process

2.5   Rotational moulding

Process description

• Raw material in the mould is heated and rotated simultaneously which forces particles to deform and melt on the walls of a female mould without the application of external pressure. The part is cooled while rotating. The mould is designed to rotate about two perpendicular axes.

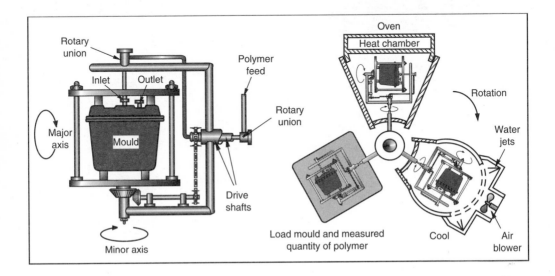

Materials

• Most thermoplastics. Polyethylene, PVC and nylon are commonly used.
• Raw material comes as finely ground powder.

Process variations

• Slush moulding: uses liquid polymers (plastisols).

Economic considerations

• Production rates of 3–50 pieces/hour, but dependent on size.
• To increase production rates three-arm carousels are often used with one mould each in the load-unload, heat and cool positions.
• Lead time several days.
• Material utilization very high. Little waste material.
• Production volumes in the range of 100–1000 are common.

- Tooling costs are low.
- Equipment costs are low.
- Labour costs are moderate.
- Finishing costs are low. Little finishing required.

Typical applications

- Tanks.
- Dust bins.
- Buckets.
- Cases.
- Footballs.

Design aspects

- Complexity limited to large, hollow, uniform wall thickness parts.
- Long, thin projections are not possible.
- Stiffening ribs and projection should have a minimum width of five times the wall thickness.
- Bosses and undercuts are possible with added cost.
- Radii should be as generous as possible.
- Metal or higher-melting point plastic inserts may be moulded in.
- Large threads can be moulded in.
- Placing of parting line important, i.e. avoid placement across critical dimensions.
- Large flat surfaces should be avoided as they tend to distort.
- Holes cannot be moulded although open-ended articles are possible.
- Draft angles are generally greater than 1°.
- Maximum section = 13 mm.
- Minimum section = 0.5 mm.
- Sizes up to 3 m^3 (>20,000-litre containers).

Quality issues

- The part is free from residual stresses.
- Surface detail is good.
- Outer surface finish of the part is a replica of the inside finish of the mould walls.
- Control of inside surface finish is not possible.
- Wall thickness is determined by the close control of the amount of raw material used.
- Dimensional variations can be large if sufficient setting time is not allowed before removal of the part.
- A process capability chart showing the achievable dimensional tolerances is given on the next page. Allowances of approximately ±0.5 mm should be added for dimensions across the parting line.
- Wall thickness tolerances are generally between ±10 to ±20% of the nominal.

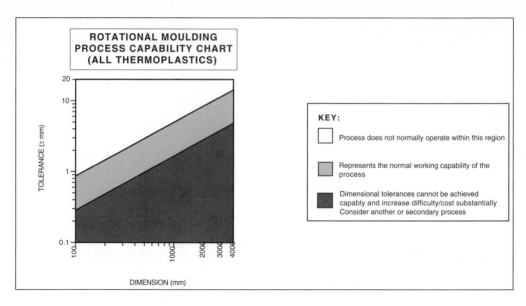

2.6 Contact moulding

Process description

- Glass fibre reinforced material (30–45% by volume) and a liquid thermosetting resin are simultaneously formed into a male or female mould and cured at room temperature or with the application of heat.

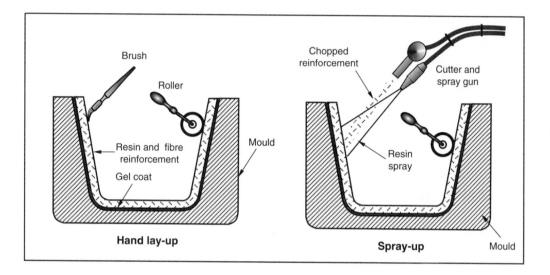

Materials

- Glass reinforced fibre in woven, continuous and chopped roving, mat and cloth forms.
- Can use partially impregnated sheet moulding compounds with the application of heat and pressure.
- Thermosetting liquid resin: commonly catalysed polyester or epoxy.

Process variations

- Hand lay-up: manual laying of fibre reinforced material and application of resin to mould to build up the thickness. Hand or roller pressure removes any trapped air.
- Variations on hand lay-up are:
  - Vacuum bag moulding: uses a rubber bag clamped over the mould. A vacuum is applied between the mould and the bag to squeeze the resin/reinforcement together removing any trapped air.
  - Pressure bag moulding: as vacuum bag moulding but pressure is applied above the bag.

- Spray lay-up: use of an air spray gun incorporating a cutter that chops continuous rovings to a controlled length before being blown into the mould simultaneously with the resin.
- Moulds can be made of wood, plaster, concrete, metal or glass fibre reinforced plastic.

Economic considerations

- Production rates are very low.
- Lead times usually short.
- Mould life is approximately 1000 parts.
- Multiple moulds incorporating heating elements should be used for higher production rates.
- Material utilization is moderate. Scrap material cannot be recycled.
- Limited amount of automation possible.
- Economical for low production runs. Can be used for one-offs.
- Tooling costs are low.
- Equipment costs generally low.
- Direct labour costs are high. Can be very labour intensive.
- Finishing costs are moderate. Some part trim is required.

Typical applications

- Hulls for boats.
- Tubs and large containers.
- Swimming pools.
- Small cabins and buildings, for example, porta-loos.
- Machine covers.
- Prototypes and mock-ups.

Design aspects

- High degree of shape complexity possible, limited only by ability to produce mould.
- Produces only one finished surface.
- Used for parts with a high surface area-to-thickness ratio.
- Inserts and bosses are possible.
- Draft angles are not required.
- Undercuts are possible with flexible moulds.
- Minimum radius = 6 mm.
- Minimum section = 1.5 mm.
- Maximum economic section = 30 mm.
- Sizes range from 0.01 to 500 m^2 in area. Maximum size depends on ability to produce mould and transport difficulties of finished part.

Quality issues

- Air entrapment and gas evolution can create a weak matrix.
- Non-reinforcing gel coat helps to create smoother mould surface and protects the moulding from moisture.
- Resin and catalyst should be accurately metered and thoroughly mixed for correct cure times.
- Excessive thickness variation can be eliminated by sufficient clamping and adequate lay-up procedures.
- Surface roughness and surface detail can be good on moulded surface.
- A process capability chart showing the achievable dimensional tolerances for hand/spray lay-up is given below.

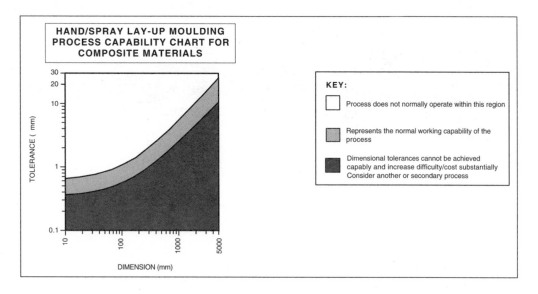

2.7 Continuous extrusion (plastics)

Process description

- The raw material is fed from a hopper into a heated barrel and pushed along a screw-type feeder where it is compressed and melts. The melt is then forced through a die of the required profile where it cools on exiting the die.

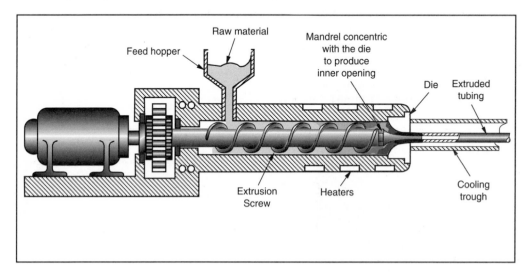

Materials

- Most plastics, especially thermoplastics, but also some thermosets.
- Elastomers.
- Raw material in pellet, granular or powder form.

Process variations

- Most extruders are equipped with a single screw, but two-screw or more extruders are available. These are able to produce coaxial fibres or tubes and multi-component sheets.
- Metal wire, strips and sections can be combined with the extrusion process using and offset die to produce plastic coatings.

Economic considerations

- Production rates are high but are dependent on size. Continuous lengths up to 60 m/min for some tube sections and profiles, up to 5 m/min for sheet and rod sections.
- Extruders are often run below their maximum speed for trouble free production.
- Can have multiple holes in die for increased production rates.
- Extruder costs increase steeply at the higher range of output.

- Lead times are dependent on the complexity of the two-dimensional die, but normally weeks.
- Material utilization is good: waste is only produced when cutting continuous section to length.
- Process flexibility is moderate: tooling is dedicated, but change-over and set-up times are short.
- Production of 1000 kg of profile extrusion is economical; 5000 kg for sheet extrusions.
- Tooling costs are generally high.
- Equipment costs are moderate to high.
- Some materials give off toxic/volatile gases during extrusion. Possible need for air extraction and washing plant which adds to equipment cost.
- Direct labour costs are low.
- Finishing costs are low.

Typical applications

- Complex profiles cut to required length.
- All types of thin-walled, open or closed profiles.
- Plastic-coated wire, cable or strips for electrical or other applications.
- Small diameter extruded bar which is cut into pellets and used for other plastic processing methods.
- Pipes, tubing and profiles.
- Polymer fibres for carpets, tyre reinforcement, clothes, ropes, etc.

Design aspects

- Dedicated to long products with uniform cross-sections.
- Cross-sections may be extremely intricate.
- Solid forms including re-entrant angles, closed or open sections.
- Section profile designed to increase assembly efficiency by integrating part consolidation features.
- Grooves, holes and inserts not parallel to the axis of extrusion must be produced by secondary operations.
- No draft angle required.
- Maximum section = 150 mm.
- Minimum section = 0.4 mm for profiles (0.02 mm for sheet).
- Sizes range from 6 mm^2 to 1800 mm wide in sheet, and from $\varnothing$1 to 150 mm in tubes and rods.

Quality issues

- The rate and uniformity of cooling are important for dimensional control because of shrinkage and distortion.
- Extrusion causes the alignment of molecules in solids.
- Die swell, (where the extruded product increases in size as it leaves the die), may be compensated for by:

- increasing haul-off rate compared with extrusion rate
- decreasing extrusion rate
- increasing the length of the die land
- decreasing the melt temperature.
• There is a tendency for powdered materials to carry air into the extruder barrel: trapped gases have a detrimental effect on both the output and the quality of the extrusion.
• Surface roughness is good to excellent.
• Process capability charts showing the achievable dimensional tolerances for various materials are given below.

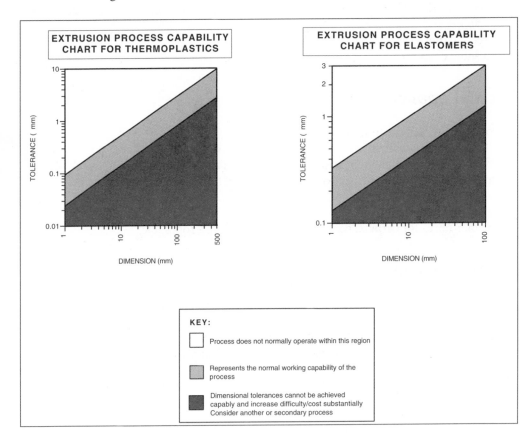

3   Forming processes

3.1 Hot forging

Process description

- Hot metal is formed into the required shape by the application of pressure or impact forces using a press or hammer in a single or a series of dies.

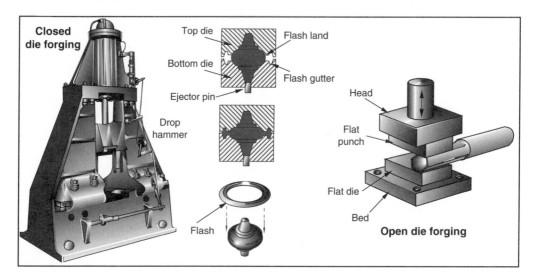

Materials

- Mainly carbon, alloy and stainless steels, aluminium, copper and magnesium alloys. Titanium alloys, nickel alloys, high alloy steels and refractory metals can also be forged.
- Forgeability of materials important, must be ductile at forging temperature. Relative forgeability is as follows, easiest to forge first: aluminium alloys, magnesium alloys, copper alloys, carbon and low alloy steels, stainless steels, titanium alloys, high alloy steels, refractory metals and nickel alloys.

Process variations

- Closed die forging: series of die impressions used to generate shape.
- Open die forging: hot material deformed between a flat punch and die. Shape and dimensions largely controlled by operator.
- Upset forging: heated metal stock gripped by dies and end pressed into desired shape.

Economic considerations

- Production rates from 1 to 300 pieces/hour, depending on size.
- Production is most economic in the production of symmetrical rough forged blanks using flat dies. Increased machining is justified by increased die life.

- Lead times are typically weeks.
- Material utilization moderate. Scrap loss depends on amount of subsequent machining required.
- Economical quantity is approximately 1000, depending on size and complexity. Can be 100 for large parts. However, more economical for high production volumes >10,000.
- In the case of open die forging: lower material utilization; machining of the final shape is necessary; slow production rate; low lead times; can be used for one-offs; high usage of skilled labour.
- Tooling costs are high.
- Equipment costs generally high.
- Direct labour costs are moderate. Some skilled operations required.
- Finishing costs are moderate. Removal of flash, cleaning and fettling important for subsequent operations.

Typical applications

- Connecting rods.
- Crankshafts.
- Axle shafts.
- Airframe components.
- Tool bodies.
- Levers.

Design aspects

- Complexity is limited by material flow through dies.
- Deep holes with small diameters are better drilled.
- Drill spots caused by die impressions aid drill centralization.
- Locating points for machining should be away from parting line due to die wear.
- Markings are possible at little expense on adequate areas that are not to be subsequently machined.
- Care should be taken with design of die geometry since cracking, mismatch, internal rupture and irregular grain flow can occur.
- Good practice to have approximately equal volumes of material both above and below the parting line.
- Placing of parting line important, i.e. avoid placement across critical dimensions.
- Corner radii and fillets should be as large as possible to aid hot metal flow.
- Avoid abrupt changes in section thickness as this causes stress concentrations on cooling.
- Inserts and undercuts are not possible.
- Machining allowances range from 0.8 to 6 mm, depending on size.
- Drafts must be added to all surfaces perpendicular to the parting line, draft angles range from 5° to 10° depending whether internal or external features.
- Minimum section = 3 mm.
- Sizes range from 10 g to 250 kg in weight.

Quality issues

- Good strength due to tough grain structure alignment.
- High fatigue resistance.
- Hot material in contact with the die too long will cause excessive wear, softening and breakage.
- Die wear and mismatch may be significant.
- Surface roughness and detail may be adequate, but secondary processing usually employed to improve the surface properties.
- Surface roughnesses is in the range 1.6–25 µm *Ra* are obtainable.
- Process capability charts showing the achievable dimensional tolerances for closed die forging using various materials are given on the next page. Note, the total tolerance on charts 1–4 is allocated $+^2/_3$, $-^1/_3$. Allowances of +0.3 to +2.8 mm should be added for dimensions across the parting line and mismatch tolerances range from 0.3 to 2.4 mm, depending on part size. Tolerances for open die forging range from ±2 to ±50 mm, depending on size of workpiece and skill of the operator.

1. CLOSED DIE FORGING PROCESS CAPABILITY CHART FOR LOW TO MEDIUM CARBON AND LOW ALLOY STEELS
(WEIGHT UP TO 1kg)

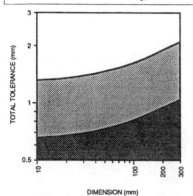

2. CLOSED DIE FORGING PROCESS CAPABILITY CHART FOR LOW TO MEDIUM CARBON AND LOW ALLOY STEELS
(WEIGHT 1→3.2kg)

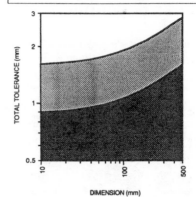

3. CLOSED DIE FORGING PROCESS CAPABILITY CHART FOR LOW TO MEDIUM CARBON AND LOW ALLOY STEELS
(WEIGHT 3.2→10kg)

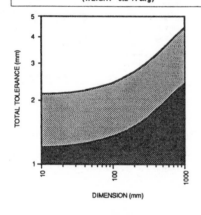

4. CLOSED DIE FORGING PROCESS CAPABILITY CHART FOR LOW TO MEDIUM CARBON AND LOW ALLOY STEELS
(WEIGHT 10→50kg)

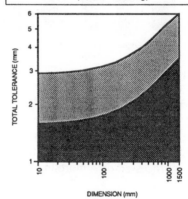

CLOSED DIE FORGING PROCESS CAPABILITY CHART FOR COPPER AND COPPER ALLOYS

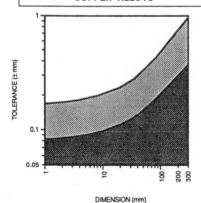

KEY:

☐ Process does not normally operate within this region

▨ Represents the normal working capability of the process

■ Dimensional tolerances cannot be achieved capably and increase difficulty/cost substantially Consider another or secondary process

3.2   Cold forming

Process description

- Various processes under the heading of cold forming tend to combine forward and backward extrusion to produce near net shaped components by the application of high pressures and forces.

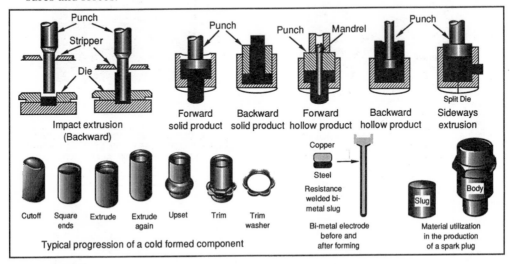

Materials

- Any ductile material at ambient temperature, including: aluminium, copper, zinc, lead and tin alloys, and low carbon steels. Also, alloy and stainless steels, nickel and titanium alloys processed on a more limited basis.

Process variations

- Impact extrusion: similar to cold extrusion but cold billet is plastically deformed by a single blow of the tool. Can be forward or backward extrusion (Hooker process).
- Cold forming: can be forward, backward or a combination of both.
- Hydrostatic extrusion: metal forced through die by high fluid pressure. Used for high strength, brittle and refractory alloy.
- Can incorporate other processes such as: cold heading, drawing, swaging, sizing and coining to produce complex parts at one station.

Economic considerations

- Production rates up to 2000 pieces/hour.
- Lead times are usually weeks.
- High utilization of material (95%). Possible material cost savings over machining can be high. Near elimination of heat treatment and machining requirements.

- Most suited to high production volumes, >100,000. Can be economical for quantities down to 5000, depending on complexity of part.
- Most applications are in the formation of symmetrical parts with solid or hollow cross sections.
- Tooling costs are high.
- Equipment costs are high.
- Direct labour costs are low.
- Finishing costs are very low.

Typical applications

- Fasteners.
- Tool sockets.
- Spark plug bodies.
- Gear blanks.
- Collapsible tubes.

Design aspects

- Complexity limited. Symmetry of the part is important: concentric, round or square cross-sections typical. Limited asymmetry possible.
- To avoid mismatch of dies, every effort should be made to balance the forces, especially on unsymmetrical parts.
- Length to diameter ratios of secondary formed back extruded parts may approach 10:1; forward extrusion unlimited.
- Any parting lines should be kept in one plane and placement across critical dimensions should be avoided.
- Can be used to process two materials simultaneously to produce parts such as steel coated copper electrodes.
- Inserts are not recommended.
- Undercuts are not possible.
- Draft angles not required.
- Maximum section ranges from 0.25 to 22 mm depending on material for impact extrusion. No limit for cold forming.
- Minimum section ranges from 0.09 to 0.25 mm depending on material.
- Sizes range from ∅1.3 to ∅150 mm depending on cold formability of material being processed.

Quality issues

- Inside shoulders require secondary processing to ensure flatness.
- Cold working offers a valuable increase in mechanical properties, including extended fatigue life.
- Concentricity of blank and punch is important in providing uniform section thickness.
- Supply of lubrication (commonly phosphate based) to the die surfaces is important in providing uniform material flow and reduced friction.

- Small quantities of sulphur, lead, phosphorus, silicon, etc., reduces the ability of ferrous metals to withstand cold working.
- Surface cracking: tearing of the surface of the part, especially with high temperature alloys, aluminium, zinc, magnesium. Control of the billet temperature, extrusion speed and friction are important.
- Pipe or fishtailing: metal flow tends to draw surface oxides and impurities towards centre of part. Governing factors are friction, temperature gradients and amount surface impurities in billets.
- Internal cracking or chevron cracking: similar to the necked region in a tensile test specimen. Governing factors are the die angle and amount of impurities in the billet.
- Surface detail excellent.
- Surface roughnesses in the range 0.1–1.6 μm *Ra* are obtainable.
- Process capability charts showing the achievable dimensional tolerances are given below.
- Dimensional tolerances for non-circular components are at least 50% greater than those shown on the charts.

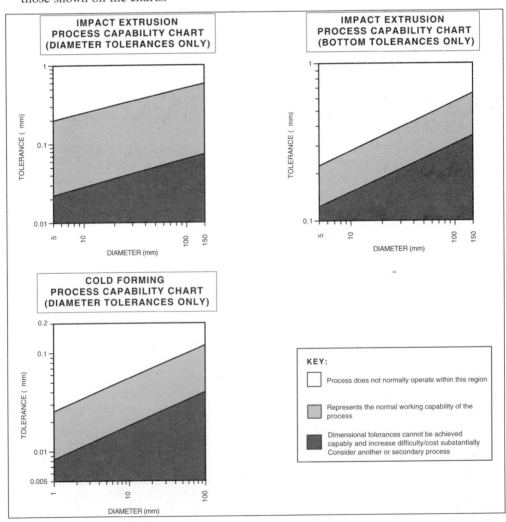

3.3 Cold heading

Process description

- Stock material is gripped in a die with usually one end protruding. The material is subsequently formed (effectively upset) by successive blows into the desired shape by a punch or a number of progressive punches. Shaping of the shank can be achieved simultaneously.

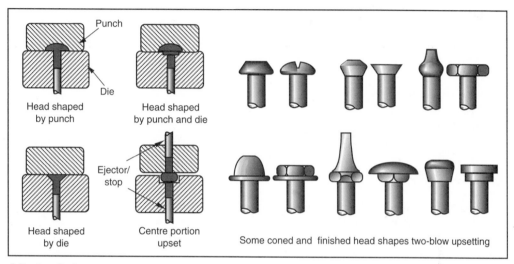

Head shaped by punch

Head shaped by punch and die

Head shaped by die

Centre portion upset

Some coned and finished head shapes two-blow upsetting

Materials

- Suitable for all ductile metals: principally, carbon steels, aluminium, copper and lead alloys. Also, alloy steel and stainless steels, zinc, magnesium and nickel alloys processed, including some precious metals.

Process variations

- Usually performed with stock material at ambient temperature (cold), but also with stock material warm or hot.
- Solid die: single stroke, double stroke, three blow, two die, progressive bolt makers, cold or hot formers – the choice is determined by the length to diameter ratio of the raw material.
- Open die: parts made by this process have wide limits and are too long for solid dies.
- Continuous rod or cut lengths of material can be supplied to the dies.
- Can incorporate other forming processes, for example: knurling, thread rolling and bending to produce complex parts at one machine.

Economic considerations

- Production rates between 35–120 pieces/minute are common.

- Lead times are relatively short due to simple dies.
- High material utilization, virtually no waste.
- Flexibility is moderate. Tooling tends to be dedicated.
- Production quantities are normally very high, >10,000.
- Tooling costs are moderate.
- Equipment costs are moderate.
- Direct labour costs are low. Process highly automated.
- Finishing costs are low: normally no finishing is required.

Typical applications

- Electronic components.
- Electrical contacts.
- Nails.
- Bolts and screws.
- Pins.
- Small shafts.

Design aspects

- Complexity limited to simple cylindrical forms with high degree of symmetry.
- Significant asymmetry difficult.
- Minimization of shank diameter and upset volume important.
- Radii should be as generous as possible.
- Threads on fasteners should be rolled wherever possible.
- Inserts are possible at added cost.
- Undercuts are produced via secondary operations.
- Machining usually not required.
- Draft angles not required.
- Sizes range from $\varnothing$0.8 and 1.5 mm long to $\varnothing$50 and 250 mm long.

Quality issues

- Cold working process gives improved mechanical properties.
- Fatigue, impact and surface strength increased giving a tough, ductile, crack resistance structure.
- Small quantities of sulphur, lead, phosphorus, silicon, etc., reduces the ability of ferrous metals to withstand cold working.
- Length to diameter ratio of protruding shank to be formed should be below 2:1 to avoid buckling.
- Internal stresses may be left at critical points.
- Surface detail is fair.
- Surface roughnesses in the range 0.8 to 6.3 μm *Ra* are obtainable.
- Process capability charts showing the achievable dimensional tolerances are given on the next page.

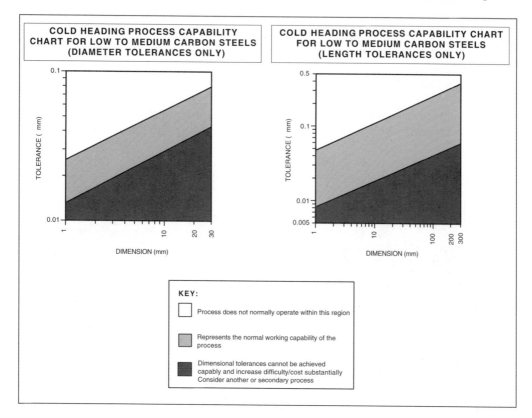

COLD HEADING PROCESS CAPABILITY CHART FOR LOW TO MEDIUM CARBON STEELS (DIAMETER TOLERANCES ONLY)

COLD HEADING PROCESS CAPABILITY CHART FOR LOW TO MEDIUM CARBON STEELS (LENGTH TOLERANCES ONLY)

TOLERANCE (mm)

DIMENSION (mm)

KEY:

Process does not normally operate within this region

Represents the normal working capability of the process

Dimensional tolerances cannot be achieved capably and increase difficulty/cost substantially Consider another or secondary process

3.4 Sheet metal shearing

Process description

- Various processes used to cut cold rolled sheet metal using punch and die sets. The most common shearing processes are: cutting, piercing, blanking and fine blanking.

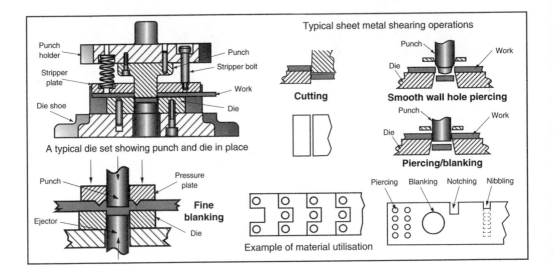

Materials

- All ductile metals available in cold-rolled sheet form, supplied flat or coiled.
- Most commonly used metals are: carbon steels, low alloy steels, stainless steels, aluminium alloys and copper alloys. Also, nickel, titanium, zinc and magnesium alloys are processed to a lesser degree.

Process variations

- Mechanical drives: faster action and more positive displacement control.
- Hydraulic drives: greater forces and more flexibility.
- Cutting: large sheets of metal are clamped and cut along a straight line.
- Piercing: removal of material from a blank, for example, a hole.
- Blanking: parts are blanked to obtain the final outside shape.
- Fine blanking: uses special clamping tooling to produce a smooth and square edged contoured blank or hole.
- Smooth wall hole piercing: special punch profiles are used to produce crack-free holes.
- Other operations include: nibbling, notching, trimming and shaving.
- Computer numerical control (CNC) common on piercing and blanking machines.

Economic considerations

- Production rates are high, up to 5000 pieces/hour on small components.
- High degree of automation possible.
- Cycle time is usually determined by loading and unloading times for stock material.
- Progressive dies can incorporate shearing and forming processes.
- Lead times can be several weeks depending on complexity and degree of automation.
- Material utilization is moderate to high, however, substantial amounts of scrap can be produced in piercing and blanking.
- Production quantities should be high for dedicated tooling, >10,000. Economical quantities can range from one for blanking and piercing to 2000 for fine blanking.
- Tooling cost moderate to high, depending on process and degree of automation.
- Equipment costs vary greatly. Low for simple guillotines to high for high speed, precision CNC presses.
- Labour costs are low to moderate depending on degree of automation.
- Finishing costs are low. Deburring and cleaning usually required.

Typical applications

- Cabinets.
- Domestic appliances.
- Aerospace and automotive components.
- Machine parts.
- Gears.
- Washers.

Design aspects

- Complex patterns of contours and holes possible in two dimensions.
- Material used dictates press forces and die clearances.
- Blanked parts should be designed to make the most use of the stock material.
- Pierced holes with their diameter greater than the material thickness should be drilled.
- Fine blanked holes with diameters 60% of the material thickness are possible.
- Holes should be spaced at least the thickness of the material away from each other.
- Maximum sheet thickness = 13 mm.
- Minimum sheet thickness = 0.1 mm.
- Maximum sheet size for cutting is 3 m and 1 m for fine blanking.

Quality issues

- Conventional hole piercing, blanking and cutting does not result in a perfectly smooth and parallel cut. Acceptable hole wall and blank edge quality may be achieved with fine blanking and piercing processes.
- Inspection and maintenance of die wear and breakage is important.
- Variations in stock material thickness and flatness should be controlled.

- Surface detail is good.
- Surface roughness values range from 0.1–12.5 μm *Ra*.
- Process capability charts showing the achievable dimensional tolerances for several sheet metal shearing processes are given below.

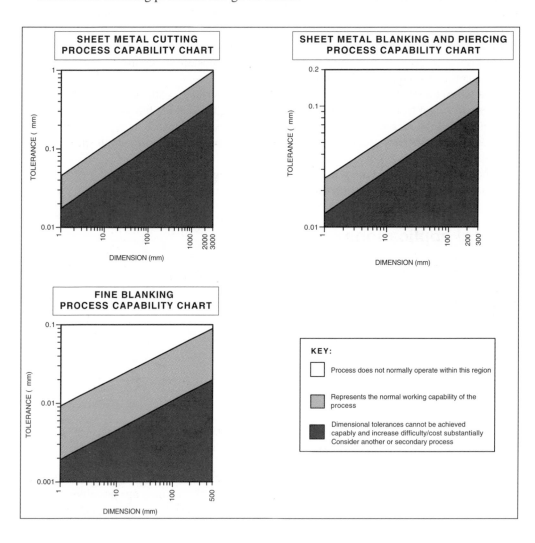

3.5	Sheet metal forming

Process description

- Various processes are used to form cold rolled sheet metal using die sets, formers, rollers, etc. The most common processes are: deep drawing, bending, stretch forming and roll forming.

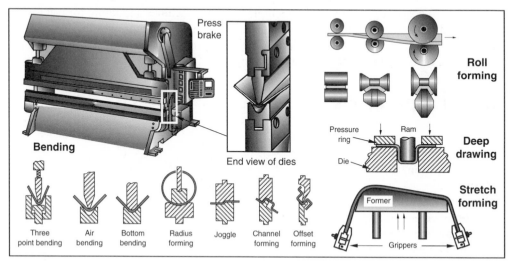

Materials

- All ductile metals available in cold rolled sheet form, supplied as blanks, flat or coiled.
- Most commonly used metals are: carbon steels, low alloy steels, stainless steels, aluminium alloys and copper alloys. Also, nickel, titanium, zinc and magnesium alloys are processed to a lesser degree.

Process variations

- Mechanical drives: faster action and more positive displacement control.
- Hydraulic drives: greater forces and more flexibility.
- Deep drawing: forming of a blank into a closed cylindrical or rectangular shaped die. Incorporating an ironing operation improves dimensional tolerances.
- Bending: deformation about a linear axis to form an angled or contoured profile.
- Stretch forming: sheet metal is clamped and stretched over a simple form tool.
- Roll forming: forming of sheet metal into complex sections using a series of rolls.
- Can incorporate initial sheet metal shearing operations.

Economic considerations

- Production rates are high, up to 3000 pieces/hour on small components.

- High degree of automation possible.
- Cycle time is usually determined by loading and unloading times for the stock material.
- Lead times vary, up to several weeks for deep drawing; could be just hours for processes like bending.
- Material utilization is moderate to high. Bending and roll forming do not produce scrap directly.
- Production quantities should be high for dedicated tooling, >10,000. Economical quantity range from one for bending to 5000 for deep drawing.
- Tooling cost moderate to high, depending on component complexity.
- Equipment costs vary greatly; low for simple bending machines, moderate for roll forming machines and high for automated deep drawing and ironing presses.
- Labour costs are low to moderate depending on degree of automation.
- Finishing costs are low. Trimming and cleaning may be required.

Typical applications

- Cabinets.
- Mounting brackets.
- Electrical fittings.
- Cans.
- Machine frames.
- Automotive and aerospace components.
- Structural members.
- Kitchen appliances and utensils.

Design aspects

- Complex forms possible: several processes may be combined to produce one component, or a series of operations used to progressively form the part.
- Working envelope of machine and uniform thickness of sheet can restrict design options.
- No inserts or re-entrant angles.
- Beading: edge of sheet bent into cavity of die. May be used to remove sharp edges.
- Hemming: edge of sheet folded over. May be used to remove sharp edges.
- Minimum bend radii are a function of material and sheet thickness.
- Minimum sheet thickness = 0.1 mm.
- Maximum sheet thickness: drawing = 12 mm, bending = 25 mm, roll/stretch forming = 6 mm.
- Sizes range from Ø2 to 600 mm for deep drawing and 10 mm to 1.5 m width for roll forming.

Quality issues

- Bending and stretch forming are limited by the onset of necking.
- The limiting drawing ratio (blank diameter/punch diameter) is between 1.6 and 2.2 for most materials. This should be observed where drawing takes place without progressive dies, otherwise excessive thinning and tearing could occur.

- Variations in stock material thickness and flatness should be controlled.
- Other problems include: spring-back (metal returns to original form) and wrinkling during drawing (comparable with forcing a circular piece of paper into a drinking glass), eliminated by adjustment of blank holder force.
- Surface detail is good.
- Surface roughness is approximately that of the stock material for forming processes.
- Process capability charts showing the achievable dimensional tolerances are given below.

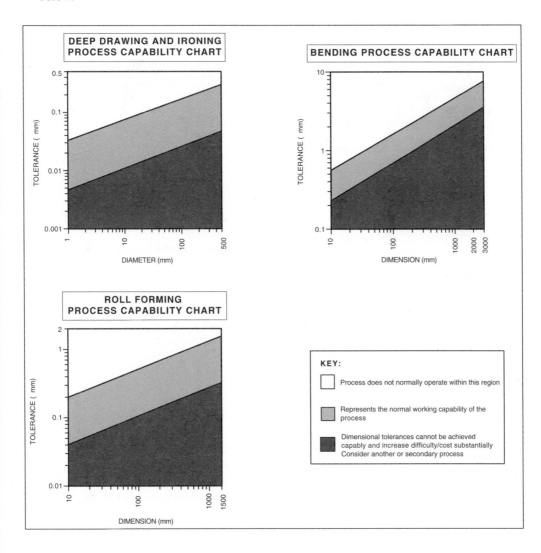

3.6   Spinning

Process description

- The forming of sheet metal by pressing it against a mandrel while it rotates using a roller or forming tool.

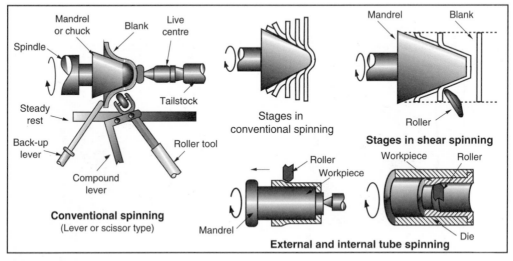

Materials

- All ductile metals that are available in sheet form. The most common metals used are: carbon steels, stainless steels, aluminium alloys, copper alloys and nickel alloys.
- Also used on a more limited basis are: zinc, magnesium, tin, lead and titanium alloys.

Process variations

- Tube spinning: cylindrical parts have their thickness reduced by spinning them on a cylindrical mandrel, either internally or externally.
- Flame spinning: the use of oxyacetylene flame permits very rapid forming on parts where size or wall thickness eliminates the use of cold spinning.
- Heavy spinning: cold material can only be flanged while hot materials can be spun into flanged, dished, spherical and conical shapes. These machines are built to special order only.
- Shear spinning: point extrusion process reduces thickness of starting blank or shape to product the final form.

Economic considerations

- Production rates are low. Typically 12–30 pieces/hour.
- Lead times are short. Simple mandrels made quickly.

- Utilization is moderate: the main losses occur in cutting blanks.
- Flexibility is high: formers are changed quickly and set-up times are low.
- Production volumes are typically less than 100. Can be used for one-offs.
- Tooling costs are low.
- Equipment costs are moderate.
- Labour costs are high. Skilled labour is needed.
- Finishing costs are low. Cleaning and trimming only required.

Typical applications

- Nose cones.
- Missile heads.
- Bells.
- Light shades.
- Cooking utensils.
- Funnels.
- Reflectors.

Design aspects

- Complexity limited to thin walled, conical, concentric shapes. Typically, the diameter is twice the depth.
- Cylindrical or cup-shaped pieces are the most difficult of the simple shapes.
- Oval or elliptical parts are possible, but expensive.
- Material thickness, bend radii, depth of spinning, diameter, steps in diameter and workability of the material are important issues in spinning.
- Stiffening beads should be formed externally rather than internally.
- Undercuts are possible, but at added cost.
- Maximum section is 75 mm for automated spinning, but approximately 6 mm for hand spinning.
- Minimum section = 0.1 mm.
- Sizes range from $\varnothing$6 to 7.5 m.

Quality issues

- Skill and experience are required to cause the metal to flow at the proper rate avoiding wrinkles and tears.
- Streamlined or smooth curves and large radii are an aid both to manufacture and improved appearance.
- Associated problems are blank development and proper feed pressure.
- Grain flow and cold working give good mechanical properties.
- Surface detail good.
- Surface roughnesses in the range 0.4–3.2 mm *Ra* are obtainable.
- A process capability chart showing the achievable dimensional tolerances is given on the next page.

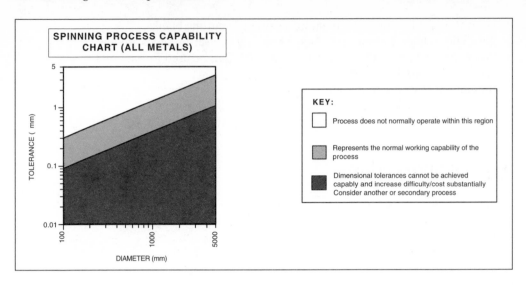

3.7   Powder metallurgy

Process description

- Die compaction of a blended powdered material into a 'green' compact which is then sintered with heat to increase the bond strength. Usually secondary operations are performed to improve dimensional accuracy, surface roughness, strength and/or porosity.

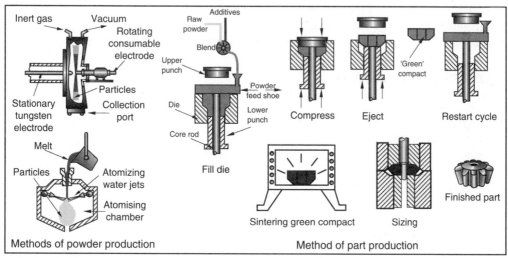

Methods of powder production   Method of part production

Materials

- All materials, typically metals and ceramics. Iron, copper alloys and refractory metals most common.
- Can process materials not formable by other methods.

Process variations

- Cold die compaction: performed at room temperature.
- Hot forging: deformation of reheated sintered compact.
- Continuous compaction: strip or sheet production (slower than conventional rolling).
- Isostatic compaction: more uniform compaction using pressurized fluid or gas. Permits undercuts and reverse tapers, but not transverse holes.
- Injection moulding: fine powder coated with thermoplastic injected into dies. Relatively complex shapes with thin walls achievable.
- Spark sintering: gives magnetic and electrical properties.
- Pressureless compaction: for porous components.
- Secondary operations include: repressing, sizing and machining.

Economic considerations

- High production rates, small parts up to 1800 pieces/hour.

- Cycle times dictated by sintering mechanisms.
- Lead times are several weeks. Dies must be carefully designed and made.
- Production quantities of >20,000 preferred, but may be economic for 5000 for simple parts.
- 100% material utilization; near net shape.
- Powders are expensive.
- Each new product requires a new set of die and punches, i.e. flexibility low.
- Tooling costs are moderate to high. Dedicated tooling.
- Equipment costs moderate to high (high when automated). Sintering equipment not dedicated.
- Labour costs are low to moderate. Some skilled labour may be required.
- Finishing costs are generally low.
- Final grinding may be more economical than sizing for very close tolerances.

Typical applications

- Cutting tools.
- Small gears.
- Lock components.
- Small arms parts.
- Bearings.
- Filters (porous).
- Machine parts.

Design aspects

- Complexity limited by powder flow through die space (powders do not follow hydro-dynamic laws) and pressing action.
- Concentric, cylindrical shapes with uniform, parallel walls preferred.
- Multiple-action tooling can be used to create complex parts.
- Complex profiles on one side only.
- Spheres approximated. Complicated radial contours possible.
- Avoid marked changes in section.
- Narrow slots, splines and sharp corners should be avoided.
- Radii should be as generous as possible.
- Chamfers preferred to radii on part edges.
- Maximum length to diameter ratio is 4:1.
- Maximum length to wall thickness ratio is 8:1.
- Grooves, cut-outs and off-axis holes perpendicular to the pressing direction cannot be produced directly.
- Inserts are possible at extra cost.
- Draft angles can be zero.
- Minimum section = 0.4 mm.
- Sizes range from 10 g to 15 kg in weight or 4 mm^2 to 0.016 m^2 in projected area.

Quality issues

- Density and strength variations in product can occur with asymmetric designs shapes. Can be minimized by die design.

- Product strength determinable by powder size, compacting pressure, sintering time and temperature, but generally, lower mechanical properties than wrought materials.
- Can give a highly porous structure, but can be controlled and used to advantage, e.g. filters, bearing lubricant impregnation.
- Generally, lower mechanical properties than wrought materials.
- Avoid sharp corners, long thin sections and large cross sectional variations.
- Remnants of contaminates at grain boundaries may act as crack initiators.
- Oxide film may impair properties of finished part, for example: chromium and high temperature super-alloys.
- Surface detail good.
- Surface roughnesses in the range 0.2 to 3.2 μm *Ra* are obtainable.
- Process capability charts showing the achievable dimensional tolerances are given below.
- Repressing and sizing improves surface roughness and dimensional accuracy.

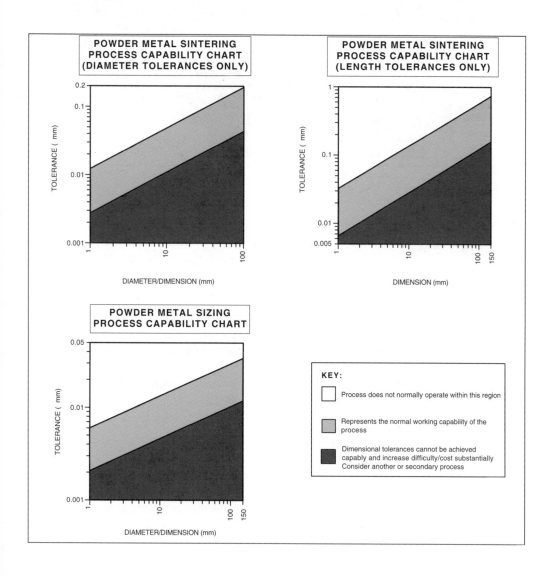

3.8 Continuous extrusion (metals)

Process description

- A billet of the raw material either hot or cold is placed into a chamber and forced through a die of the required profile with a ram.

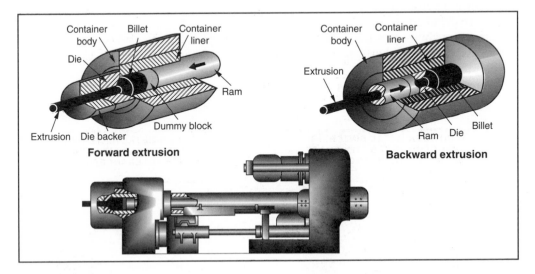

Materials

- Most ductile metals, for example: aluminium, copper and magnesium alloys. To a lesser degree: zinc, lead, tin, nickel and titanium alloys, and carbon steels are processed.

Process variations

- Forward extrusion: billet extruded by ram from behind.
- Backward extrusion: billet displaced by advancing ram with die attached to front and extrudate travels through centre of ram. Limited to short lengths only. Similar to Hooker process.
- Cold extrusion: increases friction and therefore processing energy, but increases dimensional accuracy. May be performed warm.

Economic considerations

- Production rates are high but are dependent on size and complexity. Continuous lengths up to 12 m/min.
- Extruders are often run below their maximum speed for trouble free production.
- Can have multiple holes in die for increased production rates and lower wear rates.
- Extruder costs increase steeply at the higher range of output.

- Lead times are dependent on the complexity of the two-dimensional die, but normally weeks.
- Material utilization is good: waste is only produced when cutting continuous section to length.
- Process flexibility is moderate: tooling is dedicated, but change-over and set-up times are short.
- Short production runs are viable if section designed with part consolidation and integral fastening in mind.
- Minimum billet size = 250 kg.
- Tooling costs are moderate.
- Equipment costs are high.
- Direct labour costs are low.
- Finishing costs are low.

Typical applications

- Complex profiles cut to required length.
- Wrought bar and sections for other processing methods.
- Window frames.
- Structural sections, corner and edge members.
- Decorative trim.

Design aspects

- Dedicated to long products with uniform cross-sections.
- Cross-section may be extremely complex.
- Difficult to control internal dimensions of hollow sections which use complex mandrels or spiders held in the die.
- Section profile designed to decrease amount of machining required and/or increase assembly efficiency by integrating part consolidation features.
- Solid forms including re-entrant angles.
- Grooves and holes not parallel to the axis of extrusion must be produced by a secondary operation.
- Use of materials other than aluminium and copper alloys can cause shape restrictions.
- Radii should be as generous as possible.
- No draft angle required.
- Maximum extrusion ratios – 40:1 for aluminium alloys, 5:1 for carbon steel.
- Maximum section = 100 mm.
- Minimum section = 1 mm.
- Sizes range from 8 to 500 mm sections, but dependent on complexity and material used.

Quality issues

- Avoid knife edges and long, unsupported projections.
- Warp and twist can be troublesome.
- Plastic working produces favourable grain structure and directional properties.

- The rate and uniformity of cooling are important for dimension control because of shrinkage and distortion.
- Die swell, (where the extruded product increases in size as it leaves the die), may be compensated for by:
  - increasing haul-off time compared with extrusion rate
  - decreasing extrusion rate
  - increasing the length of the die land
  - decreasing the extrusion temperature.
- Surface detail is good to excellent. Surface roughnesses in the range 0.4 to 12.5 μm *Ra* are obtainable.
- Process capability charts showing the achievable dimensional tolerances are given below.
- Straightness obtainable is generally 0.3 mm/m.

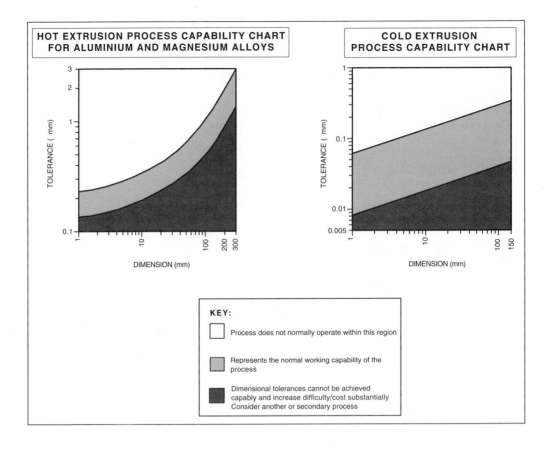

4 Machining processes

4.1   Automatic and manual turning and boring

Process description

- The removal of material by chip processes using sequenced or simultaneous machining operations on cut to length bar or coiled bar stock. The stock can be automatically or manually fed into the machine.

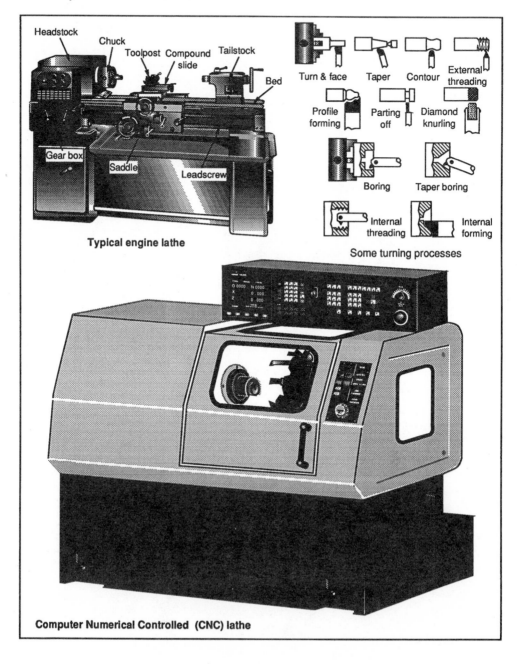

Typical engine lathe

Some turning processes

Turn & face   Taper   Contour   External threading

Profile forming   Parting off   Diamond knurling

Boring   Taper boring

Internal threading   Internal forming

Computer Numerical Controlled (CNC) lathe

Materials

- All metals (mostly free machining), some plastics, elastomers and some ceramics.

Process variations

- Manually operated machines include: bench lathes (can machine non-standard shape parts) and turret lathes (limited to standard stock material).
- Automatic machines: fully or semi-automated. Follow operations activated by mechanisms on the machine.
- Automatic bar machines: used mainly for the production of screws and similar parts. Single spindle, multiple spindle and swiss-types are available.
- CNC machines: movement and control of tool, headstock and saddle are performed by a computer program via stepper motors.
- Machining centres: fully automated, integrated turning, boring, drilling and milling machines capable of performing a wide range of operations.
- Extensive range of cutting tool geometries and tool materials available.

Economic considerations

- Production rates range from 1 to 60 pieces/hour for manual machining, 10 to >1000 pieces/hour for automatic machining.
- Lead times vary from short to moderate.
- Material utilization is poor. Large quantities of chips generated which can be recycled.
- Flexibility is low to moderate for automatic machines: change over and set-up times can be many hours. Manual machines are very flexible.
- Economical quantity is >1000 for automatic machines and production volumes of >100,000 are common. Manual and CNC machining are commonly used for small production runs, but can also be economic for one-offs.
- Tooling costs are moderate to high for automatic machines, low for manual.
- Equipment costs are high for automatic/CNC machines. Moderate for manual machining.
- Direct labour costs are high for manual machining, low to moderate for automatic/CNC machining.
- Finishing costs are low. Only cleaning and deburring required.

Typical applications

- Any component with rotational symmetrical elements requiring close tolerances.
- Non-standard shapes requiring secondary operations.
- Shafts.
- Screws and fasteners.
- Transmission components.
- Engine parts.

Design aspects

- Complexity limited to elements with rotational symmetry.
- Little opportunity for part consolidation.
- Can perform many different operations in a logical sequence on the same machine.
- Potential for linking with CAD very high.
- Reduce machining operations to a minimum (for simplicity and lower cycle time).
- Fillet corners and chamfer edges where possible to increase tool life.
- Holes should be drilled with a standard drill point at the bottom for economy.
- Required number of full threads should always be specified.
- Leading threads on both male and female work should be chamfered to assure efficient assembly.
- Special attachments make auxiliary operations possible, for example, drilling and milling perpendicular to the length of the work.
- Some special machines allow larger pieces but then operations are restricted.
- Sizes range from $\varnothing 0.5$ to 2 m for manual and CNC machining. Automatic machines usually have a capacity of less than $\varnothing 60$ mm.

Quality issues

- Machinability of the material to be processed is an important issue with regards to: surface roughness, surface integrity, tool life, cutting forces and power requirements. Machinability is expressed in terms of a 'machinability index'* for the material.
- Multiple set-ups can be a source of variability.
- Selection of appropriate cutting tool, coolant, feed rate, depth of cut and cutting speed with respect to material to be machined is important.
- Regular inspection of cutting tool condition and material specification is important for minimum variability.
- Surface detail good to excellent.
- Surface roughness values in the range from 0.05 to 25 mm *Ra* are obtainable.
- Process capability charts showing the achievable dimensional tolerances for turning/boring (using conventional and diamond tipped cutting tools) are given on the next page. Note, the tolerances on these charts are greatly influenced by the machinability index for the material used.

*Machinability index for a material is expressed as a percentage based on the relative ease of machining a material with respect to free cutting mild steel which is 100% and taken as the standard.

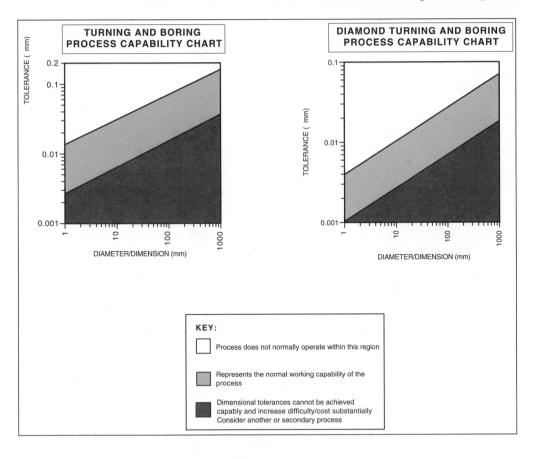

4.2 Milling

Process description

- The removal of material by chip processes using multiple point cutting tools of various shapes to generate flat surfaces or profiles on a workpiece of regular or irregular section.

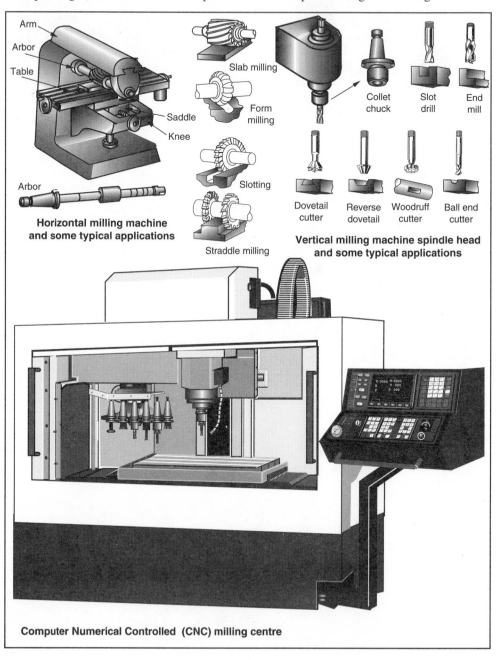

Horizontal milling machine and some typical applications

Vertical milling machine spindle head and some typical applications

Computer Numerical Controlled (CNC) milling centre

Materials

- All metals (mostly free machining) and some plastics and ceramics.

Process variations

- Horizontal milling: axis of cutter rotation is parallel to surface of workpiece. Includes slab milling, form milling, slotting, gang milling and slitting. Can be either up-cut or down-cut milling.
- Vertical milling: axis of cutter rotation is perpendicular to surface of workpiece. Includes face milling, slotting, dovetail and woodruff milling.
- CNC machines: movement and control of tool, headstock and bed are performed by a computer program via stepper motors.
- Extensive range of cutting tool geometries and tool materials available.

Economic considerations

- Production rates range from 1 to 100 pieces/hour.
- Lead times vary from short to moderate. Reduced by CNC.
- Material utilization is poor. Large quantities of chips generated.
- Recycling of waste material possible but difficult.
- Flexibility is high. Little dedicated tooling.
- Production volumes are usually low. Can be used for one-offs.
- Tooling costs are moderate depending on degree of automation.
- Equipment costs are moderate to high.
- Direct labour costs are moderate to high. Skilled labour required.
- Finishing costs are low. Cleaning and deburring required.

Typical applications

- Any standard or non-standard shapes requiring secondary operations.
- Aircraft wing spars.
- Engine blocks.
- Pump components.
- Machine components.
- Gears.

Design aspects

- Complexity limited by cutter profiles and workpiece orientation.
- Potential for linking with CAD very high.
- Chamfered edges preferred to radii.
- Use standard sizes and shapes for milling cutter wherever possible.
- Special attachments make auxiliary operations possible, for example, gear cutting using an indexing head.

- Minimum section less than 1 mm, but see below.
- Minimum size limited by ability to clamp workpiece to milling machine bed.
- Maximum size approximately 5 m long, but dependent on size of machine bed.

Quality issues

- Machinability of the material to be processed is an important issue with regards to: surface roughness, surface integrity, tool life, cutting forces and power requirements. Machinability is expressed in terms of a 'machinability index' for the material.
- Rigidity of milling cutter, workpiece and milling machine important in preventing deflections during machining.
- Selection of appropriate cutting tool, coolant, depth of cut, feed rate and cutting speed with respect to material to be machined is important.
- Regular inspection of cutting tool condition and material specification is important for minimum variability.
- Surface detail good.
- Surface roughness values in the range 0.2 to 25 μm *Ra* are obtainable.
- A process capability chart showing the achievable dimensional tolerances for milling is given below. Note, the tolerances on this chart are greatly influenced by the machinability index for the material used.

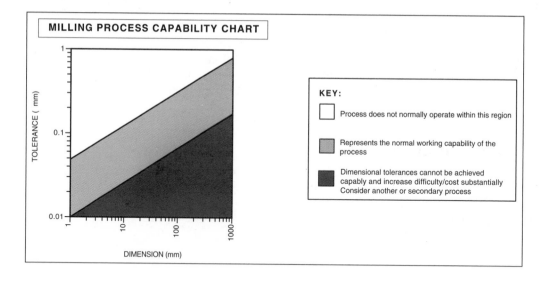

4.3 Planing and shaping

Process description

- The removal of material by chip processes using single point cutting tools that move in a straight line parallel to the workpiece with either the workpiece reciprocating in planing or the tool reciprocating in shaping. Simplest of all machining processes.

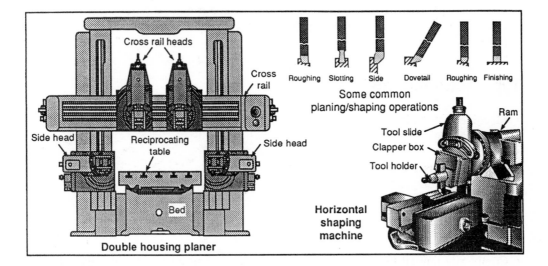

Materials

- All metals (mostly free machining).

Process variations

- Double housing planer: closed gantry carrying several tool heads.
- Open side planer: open gantry to accommodate large workpieces carrying usually one tool-head.
- Horizontal shaping: includes push-cut and pull-cut.
- Vertical shaping: includes slotters and key-seaters.
- Wide range of cutting tool geometries and tool materials available.

Economic considerations

- Production rates range from 1 to 50 pieces/hour.
- Lead times vary from short to moderate.
- Material utilization is poor. Large quantities of chips generated which can be recycled.
- Flexibility is high. Little dedicated tooling and set-up times are generally short.

- On larger parts, the elapsed time between cutting stokes can be long making the process inefficient. Can be improved by having the cutting stoke in both directions, using several cutting tools and/or machining several parts at once.
- Other processes, for example, milling or broaching, may be more economical for larger production runs of smaller parts.
- Planing machines are usually integrated with milling machines to make them more flexible.
- Least economical quantity is one. Production volumes are usually very low.
- Tooling costs are low.
- Equipment costs are moderate to high.
- Direct labour costs are high to moderate. Skilled labour may be required.
- Finishing costs are moderate. Normally requires some other machining operations for finishing.

Typical applications

- Machine tools beds.
- Large castings.
- Die blocks.
- Key-seats, slots and notches.
- Large gear teeth.

Design aspects

- Complexity limited by nature of process, i.e. straight profiles, slots and flat surfaces along length of workpiece.
- As many surfaces as possible should lie in the same plane for machining.
- Rigidity of workpiece design important in preventing vibration.
- Minimum section less than 2 mm, but see below.
- Minimum size limited by ability to clamp workpiece to machine bed.
- Maximum size approximately 25 m long in planing, and 2 m long in shaping.

Quality issues

- Machinability of the material to be processed is an important issue with regards to: surface roughness, surface integrity, tool life, cutting forces and power requirements. Machinability is expressed in terms of a 'machinability index' for the material.
- Adequate clearance should be provided for to prevent rubbing and chipping of the cutting tool on return strokes.
- Cutting tools require chip breakers for ductile materials because the strokes can be long during machining and the swarf may tangle and pose a safety hazard.
- Selection of appropriate cutting tool, coolant, depth of cut, feed rate and cutting speed with respect to material to be machined is important.
- Can produce large, accurate, distortion free surfaces due to low cutting forces and low local heat generation.

- Surface detail fair.
- Surface roughness values in the range from 0.4 to 25 mm *Ra* are obtainable.
- A process capability chart showing the achievable dimensional tolerances is given below. Note, the tolerances on this chart are greatly influenced by the machinability index for the material used.

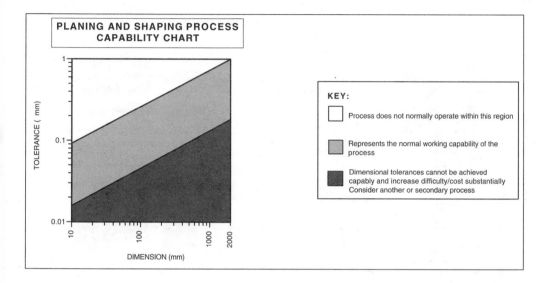

PLANING AND SHAPING PROCESS
CAPABILITY CHART

KEY:

Process does not normally operate within this region

Represents the normal working capability of the process

Dimensional tolerances cannot be achieved capably and increase difficulty/cost substantially Consider another or secondary process

4.4   Drilling

Process description

- The removal of material by chip processes using rotating tools of various types with two or more cutting edges to produce cylindrical holes in a workpiece.

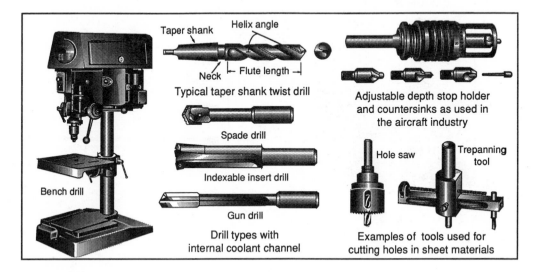

Materials

- All metals (mostly free machining) and some plastics and ceramics.

Process variations

- Variations on the basic drilling machine include: bench, column, radial arm, gang, multiple spindle, turret and CNC-controlled turret.
- Variations on the basic drill types include: twist drill (either three flute, taper shank, bit shank and straight flute), gun drills, spade drill, indexible insert drill, ejector drill, hole saw, trepanning and solid boring drill.
- Variations on conventional drill point geometry are aimed at reducing cutting forces and self-centring capability and include: four facet, helical, Racon, Bickford and split point.
- Wide range of cutting tool materials available. Titanium nitride coatings are also used to increase tool life.
- Drilling can also be performed on lathes, milling machines and machining centres.
- Spot facing, counterboring and countersinking are related drilling processes.

Economic considerations

- Production rates range from 10 to 500 pieces/hour.
- Lead times vary from short to moderate. Reduced by automation.
- Material utilization is very poor. Large quantities of chips generated which can be recycled.
- Flexibility is high. Little dedicated tooling and generally short set-up times.
- Drill jigs facilitate the reproduction of accurate holes on large production runs.
- Production volumes are usually low to moderate. Can be used for one-offs.
- Production costs significantly reduced with multiple spindle machines when used on large production runs.
- Tooling costs are low.
- Equipment costs are low to moderate.
- Direct labour costs are low to moderate. Low operator skill required.
- Finishing costs are low. Cleaning and deburring required.

Typical applications

- Any component requiring cylindrical holes, either blind or through.
- Engine blocks.
- Pump components.
- Machine components.

Design aspects

- Complexity limited to cylindrical blind or through hole.
- Use standard sizes wherever possible.
- Faces to be drilled are usually required to be perpendicular to the drilling direction unless spot faced and adequate clearance should be provided for.
- Exit surfaces should be perpendicular to hole.
- Through holes preferred to blind holes.
- Allowances should be made for drill point depths in blind holes.
- Flat bottomed holes should be avoided.
- Centre drilling usually required before drilling unless special drill point geometry used.
- Holes with a length to diameter ratio of greater than 70 have been produced but problems with hole straightness, coolant supply and chip removal may cause drill breakage.
- Sizes range from ∅0.1 mm for twist drills to ∅250 mm for trepanning.

Quality issues

- Machinability of the material to be processed is an important issue with regards to: surface roughness, surface integrity, tool life, cutting forces and power requirements. Machinability is expressed in terms of a 'machinability index' for the material.
- Hard spots, oxide layers and poor surfaces can cause drill point to blunt or break.

- Accurate re-grinding of the drill point geometry is required to maintain correct hole size and balance cutting forces to avoid drill breakage.
- Rigidity of drilling machine, workpiece and drill holder and concentricity of drill spindle important in preventing oversize holes.
- Selection of appropriate drill geometry (including relief and rake angles), coolant, size of cut/hole, feed rate and cutting speed with respect to material to be machined is important.
- Drills may require chip breakers for ductile materials to efficiently remove swarf from cutting area.
- Surface detail fair.
- Surface roughness values in the range from 0.4 to 12.5 mm *Ra* are obtainable.
- A process capability chart showing the achievable dimensional tolerances is given below. Note, the tolerances on this chart are greatly influenced by the machinability index for the material used.

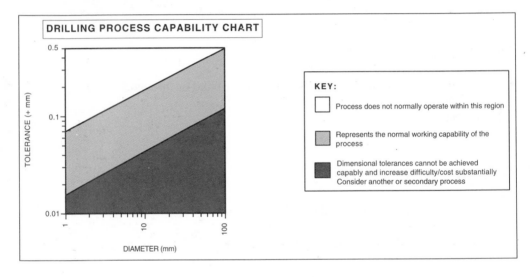

4.5   Broaching

Process description

- The removal of material by chip processes using a multiple point cutting tool which is pushed or pulled across the workpiece surface, and with successively deeper cuts, gradually generates the desired profile in a single pass.

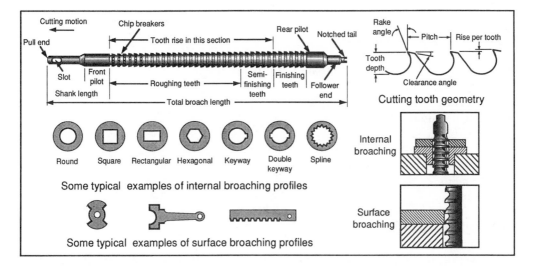

Materials

- All metals (mostly free machining).

Process variations

- Horizontal, vertical or rotary broaching machines with push and/or pull capability.
- Broaching tools can be single or combination types, internal or external, performing either roughing or finishing operations.
- Some indexible insert broaches are available for surface broaching and titanium nitride coatings on are also used to increase tool life.

Economic considerations

- Production rates up to 400 pieces/hour.
- To improve production rates, many parts can be machined at once, called stacking. Stacking is best suited to internal features.
- Automation possible to improve production rates.
- Lead times are moderate.
- Material utilization is poor. Large quantities of chips generated which can be recycled.

- Flexibility is high. Little dedicated tooling and set-up times are generally short.
- Accurate re-grinding of the broaching tool is required on large production runs, which uses expensive fixtures and grinding machines.
- Production volumes are usually very high, >3000.
- Tooling costs are high. Broaching tools are very expensive due to their complexity and the economics of this process must be carefully studied on this basis.
- Equipment costs are low to moderate.
- Direct labour costs are low to moderate. Some skilled labour may be required.
- Finishing costs are low. Some deburring may be required.

Typical applications

- Many regular or irregular, internal or external profiles.
- Turbine blade root forms.
- Connecting rods.
- Rifling on gun barrels.
- Flat surfaces.
- Key seats and slots.
- Splines, both straight and helical.
- Gear teeth.

Design aspects

- Complexity limited by nature of process, i.e. straight, curved and complex profiles, slots and flat surfaces along length of workpiece.
- Part design should allow for sufficient clamping area and clearance for broaching tool.
- A hole is initially required for internal broaching for broaching tool access. This can be achieved by either punching, boring or drilling the blank.
- Ideally, between 0.5 and 6 mm should be removed by the broaching tool on any one surface.
- More than one surface can be cut simultaneously.
- Workpiece must be strong enough to withstand the pressure of continuous cutting action of broach.
- Large surfaces, blind holes and sharp corners should be avoided.
- Chamfers are preferred to radiused corners.
- Minimum stroke = 25 mm.
- Maximum stroke = 3 m.

Quality issues

- Machinability of the material to be processed is an important issue with regards to: surface roughness, surface integrity, tool life, cutting forces and power requirements. Machinability is expressed in terms of a 'machinability index' for the material.
- For materials with high surface hardness, the first tooth on the broach should cut beneath this layer to improve tool life.

- Soft or non-uniform materials may tear during machining.
- Adequate clearance should be provided for to prevent rubbing and chipping of the broaching tool on return strokes.
- Broaching tools may require chip breakers for very ductile materials to efficiently remove swarf from cutting area.
- Selection of appropriate cutting tool material, coolant, depth of cut per tooth and cutting speed with respect to material to be machined is important.
- Surface detail excellent.
- Surface roughness values in the range from 0.4 to 6.3 μm *Ra* are obtainable.
- A process capability chart showing the achievable dimensional tolerances is given below. Note, the tolerances on this chart are greatly influenced by the machinability index for the material used.

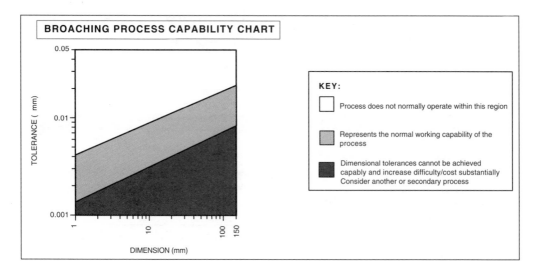

4.6 Reaming

Process description

- The removal of small amounts of material by chip processes using tools of various types with several cutting edges to improve the accuracy, roundness and surface finish of existing cylindrical holes in a workpiece. The tool or the work can rotate relative to each other.

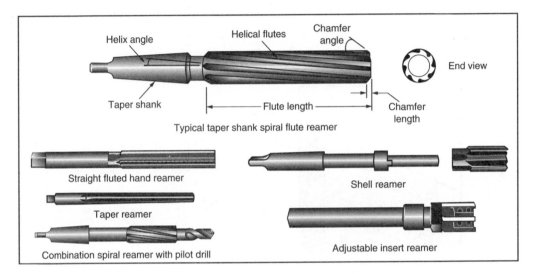

Materials

- All metals (mostly free machining).

Process variations

- No special machines are used for reaming. Reaming can be performed on drilling machines, lathes, milling machines and machining centres, or by hand.
- Basic reamer types include: hand (straight and tapered), machine (rose and fluted), shell, expansion, adjustable and indexible insert reamers. Titanium nitride coatings are sometimes used to increase tool life. Combination drills and reamers are also available.

Economic considerations

- Production rates range from 10 to 500 pieces/hour.
- Lead times vary from short to moderate. Reduced by automation.
- Minimum amount of material removed.
- Flexibility is high. Little dedicated tooling and generally short set-up times.
- Production volumes are usually low to moderate.

- Can be used for one-offs.
- Production costs significantly reduced with multiple spindle machines.
- Tooling costs are low.
- Equipment costs are low.
- Direct labour costs are low to moderate. Low operator skill required.
- Finishing costs are low. Cleaning and deburring required.

Typical applications

- Any component requiring accurate, cylindrical holes with good surface finish, either blind or through after a primary hole making operation.

Design aspects

- Complexity limited to cylindrical blind or through holes.
- Ideally, reaming allowances should be between 0.1 mm and 0.5 mm.
- Allowances should be made for reamer end chamfers and slight taper on some reamers when machining blind holes.
- Use standard sizes wherever possible.
- Through holes preferred to blind holes.
- Sizes range from ∅3 to 100 mm.

Quality issues

- Machinability of the material to be processed is an important issue with regards to: surface roughness, surface integrity, tool life, cutting forces and power requirements. Machinability is expressed in terms of a 'machinability index' for the material.
- Any misalignment between workpiece and reamer will cause chatter, oversize holes and bell-mouthing of hole entrance. Piloted reamers ensure alignment of the workpiece and reamer.
- Most accurate holes are centre drilled, drilled, bored and reamed to finished size.
- Proper maintenance and reconditioning of reamers is required to maintain correct hole size and surface finish requirements. To work efficiently, a reamer must have all its teeth cutting.
- Pick-up or galling are caused by too much material being removed by the reamer.
- Selection of appropriate reamer geometry (including relief and rake angles), coolant (if required), size of hole, feed rate and cutting speed with respect to material to be machined is important. Reaming is performed at one-third the speed and two-thirds the feed rate of drilling for optimum conditions.
- Surface detail good.
- Decreasing feed rate improves surface finish.
- Surface roughness values in the range from 0.4 to 6.3 μm *Ra* are obtainable.
- A process capability chart showing the achievable dimensional tolerances is given on the next page. Note, the tolerances on this chart are greatly influenced by the machinability index for the material used.

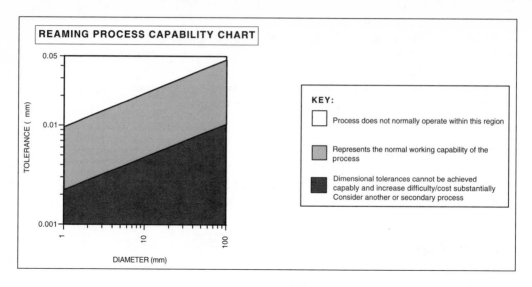

4.7   Grinding

Process description

- The removal of material by the action of an abrasive spinning wheel on rotating or reciprocating workpiece.

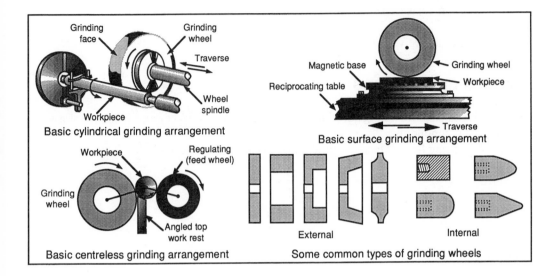

Grinding face • Grinding wheel • Traverse • Wheel spindle • Workpiece
Basic cylindrical grinding arrangement

Magnetic base • Reciprocating table • Grinding wheel • Workpiece • Traverse
Basic surface grinding arrangement

Workpiece • Regulating (feed wheel) • Grinding wheel • Angled top work rest
Basic centreless grinding arrangement

External • Internal
Some common types of grinding wheels

Materials

- All hard materials. Not suitable for flexible materials.

Process variations

- Surface grinding: workpiece is mounted on a reciprocating bed and a rotating abrasive wheel fed across the surface.
- Cylindrical grinding: rotating abrasive wheel fed along the periphery of a slower rotating cylindrical workpiece. Also includes: thread, form and plunge grinding.
- Internal grinding: small rotating abrasive wheel fed into the bore of a cylindrical rotating workpiece.
- Centreless grinding: workpiece is supported on a work rest blade and ground between two wheels, one of which is a regulating wheel operating at 1/20 the speed of the other.
- CNC machines: movement and control of abrasive wheel and workpiece are performed by a computer program via stepper motors.
- Extensive range of abrasive wheel geometries, abrasive materials, grain size, hardness grading and bond types are available.

Economic considerations

- Production rates range from 1 to 1000 pieces/hour.
- Lead times vary from short to moderate.
- Material utilization is poor. Difficult to recycle waste material.
- Flexibility of grinding is high.
- Turning can compete with grinding in some situations.
- Suitable for all quantities.
- Tooling costs are moderate depending on degree of automation.
- Equipment costs are moderate to high.
- Direct labour costs range from high to low depending on degree of automation and part complexity.
- Finishing costs are very low. Cleaning required.

Typical applications

- Grinding is used for the generation of basic geometric surfaces and finishing of a wide range of components.
- Parts requiring fine surface roughness and/or close tolerances.
- Bearing surfaces.
- Valve seats.
- Gears.
- Cams.

Design aspects

- Complexity limited to nature of workpiece surface, i.e. cylindrical or flat, unless profiled wheels and/or special machines are used.
- Grinding should be used to remove the minimum amount of material.
- Surface features should be kept simple to avoid frequent dressing of the wheel.
- Fillets and corner radii should be as liberal as possible.
- Deep holes and recesses should be avoided.
- Parts should be mounted securely to avoid deflections as high forces can be generated during the grinding process.
- May not be suitable for delicate workpieces.
- For best results use the largest wheel possible for the relevant workpiece.
- Minimum section = 0.5 mm.
- Sizes range from ∅0.5 mm to 2 m for cylindrical grinding. Maximum size for surface grinding approximately 6 m in length. Less than ∅1 m for centreless grinding.

Quality issues

- Interruptions on the workpiece surface, for example, key seats, may cause vibration and chatter.
- Unit pressures vary with area of contact: high pressures use hard grade, fine grit abrasive wheels.

- Residual stresses may remain in the workpiece due to temperature changes and gradients: this may be critical in heat sensitive applications.
- The final size of the workpiece is determined by the speed of response of the gauging system and the forces built up in machine as a result of cutting loads.
- Gauging may be contact or non-contact this will probably be dictated by the part.
- The properties of the wheel may change in the course of the process.
- The dressing of the wheel with grinding fluid is very important for chip removal and cooling of the workpiece.
- Grinding wheels need careful storage and to be visually inspected for cracks before use.
- Surface roughness is controlled by the wheel grading, wheel condition, feed rate at finish size and cleanliness of the cutting fluid.
- Surface detail excellent.
- Surface roughness values in the range from 0.025 to 6.3 μm *Ra* are obtainable.
- Process capability charts showing the achievable dimensional tolerances for surface and cylindrical grinding are given below.

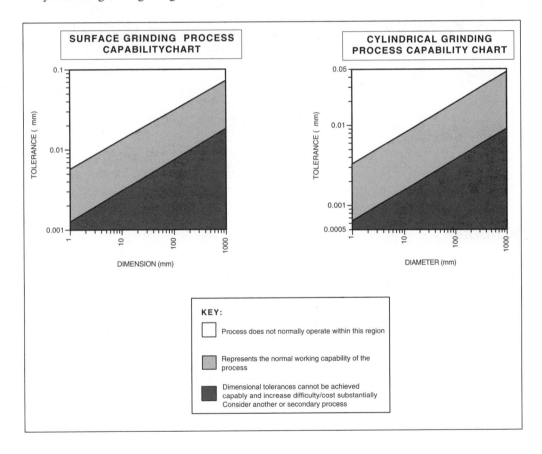

4.8   Honing

Process description

- The removal of small amounts of material by floating segmented abrasive stones mounted on an expanding mandrel which rotates with low rotary speed and reciprocates along the surface of the workpiece.

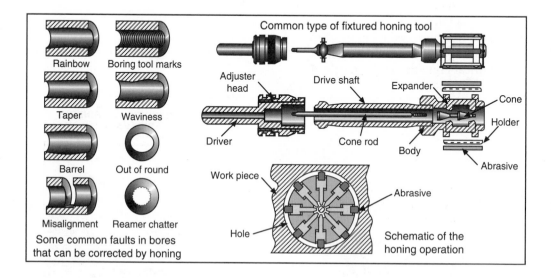

Some common faults in bores that can be corrected by honing

Schematic of the honing operation

Materials

- All materials, including some ceramics and plastics.

Process variations

- Horizontal and vertical honing machines with single or multiple spindles, with either short or long stroke capability.
- Honing can also be performed on lathes and drilling machines.
- Internal and external cylindrical surfaces are honed commonly. Also, spherical, toroidal and flat surfaces can be honed, but are less common applications.
- Automation aspects include in-process gauging and adaptive control to optimize cutting conditions and control accuracy.
- Single stroke bore finishing and superfinishing using 'superabrasives' (diamond, CBN) are related processes.
- Large range of stone geometries, abrasive materials, grain size, hardness grading and bond types are available.
- Workpieces can be manually presented to honing mandrel.

Economic considerations

- Production rates range from 10 to 1000 pieces/hour, depending on number of spindles. Typically 60 pieces/hour for single spindle machines.
- Lead times are short.
- Very little material removed.
- Suitable for all quantities.
- Tooling costs vary depending on degree of automation and size.
- Equipment costs are moderate.
- Direct labour costs are moderate. Skill level required is moderate to high (manual).
- Finishing costs are very low. Cleaning only required.

Typical applications

- Any component where superior accuracy, surface finish and/or improvement of geometric features is required on cylindrical features.
- Bearing surfaces.
- Pin and dowel holes.
- Engine cylinder bores.
- Rifle bores.

Design aspects

- Honing is performed to remove the minimum amount of material, usually between 0.02 and 0.2 mm.
- Complexity limited to nature of workpiece surface, i.e. cylindrical (internal and external), spherical or flat.
- Honing logically follows the grinding process to produce precision surfaces.
- Surface features should be kept simple.
- Chamfers are required on entrance to bores to facilitate easy access of honing tool.
- Blind holes should have undercuts.
- For small holes $< \varnothing15$ mm, the maximum length that can be honed is 20 times the diameter of the hole. For best results, a length to diameter ratio of one is recommended.
- Maximum length for large holes is 12 m.
- Sizes range from $\varnothing6$ to 750 mm for cylindrical honing.

Quality issues

- Interruptions on the workpiece surface, for example, key seats and holes, reduce the quality of finish. Can be offset by increasing rotary speed of honing stone.
- The process has the ability to correct geometrical inaccuracies, for example, bell-mouthing, barrelling, tapers and waviness in holes, as well as removing machining marks.
- Surface finish and accuracy is controlled by the stone grain size, feed pressure, area of contact, coolant access, stroke length, rotary speed and stone reciprocation speed, which when optimized ensure breakdown of the stone and good self-dressing characteristics.

- Little heat generated at surface, therefore, component surface characteristics not altered.
- Surface detail excellent.
- Surface roughness values in the range from 0.025 to 1.6 μm *Ra* are obtainable.
- Softer materials tend to give inferior surface finish to hard materials.
- A process capability chart showing the achievable dimensional tolerances is given below.

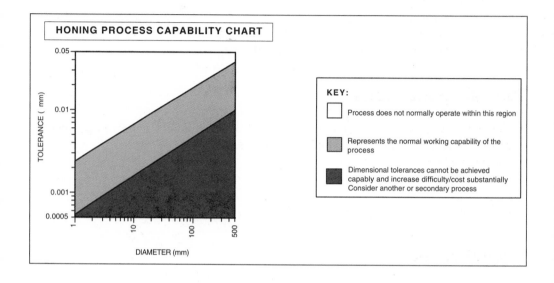

4.9   Lapping

Process description

- The removal of very small amounts of material by the relative motion of fine abrasive particles embedded in a soft material (lap), with the aid of a lubricating and carrier fluid.

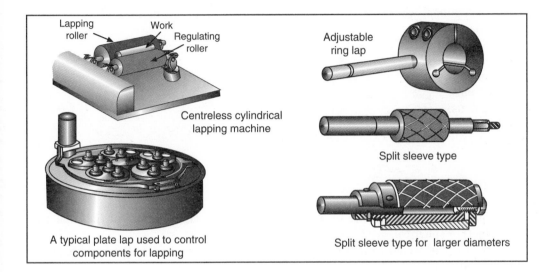

Lapping roller   Work   Regulating roller

Centreless cylindrical lapping machine

A typical plate lap used to control components for lapping

Adjustable ring lap

Split sleeve type

Split sleeve type for larger diameters

Materials

- All materials, but workpieces of low hardness can present problems (see below).

Process variations

- Hand lapping: operator moves the workpiece over a grooved surface plate in an irregular rotary motion, turning the part frequently.
- Machine lapping: horizontal and vertical lapping machines with variety of floating work holding devices that can carry many parts at once.
- Centreless lapping: used for internal and external cylindrical, spherical and contoured surfaces.
- Range of lap materials, abrasive materials, grain size and carrier fluids are available.

Economic considerations

- Production rates range from 10 to 3000 pieces/hour, depending on level of automation.
- Lead times are short.

- Very little material removed.
- Suitable for all quantities.
- Tooling costs vary depending on degree of automation and size.
- Equipment costs are moderate.
- Direct labour costs are low to moderate. High skill level required for hand lapping.
- Finishing costs are very low. Cleaning only required.

Typical applications

- Any component where superior surface finish is required on flat, cylindrical or contoured surfaces.
- Bearing surfaces.
- Gauge blocks.
- Piston rings.
- Piston pins.
- Valve seats.
- Glass lenses.
- Gears.

Design aspects

- Complexity limited to nature of workpiece surface, i.e. flat, cylindrical (internal and external) or spherical.
- Lapping is performed to remove the minimum amount of material, usually between 0.005 and 0.01 mm.
- Lapping should not be specified if the surface finish on the component is not critical and can be produced by other processes.
- Lapping logically follows the grinding or honing process to produce precision surfaces.
- Parts required to provide lapping pressure under their own weight should have a low centre of gravity and be stable.
- Surface features should be kept simple.
- Sizes range from 1 to 500 mm for flat lapping.
- Centreless lapping sizes range from $\varnothing 0.75$ to 300 mm. Maximum lengths are ≥ 4 m for up to $\varnothing 75$ mm.

Quality issues

- Soft materials are difficult to lap due to abrasive particles becoming embedding in workpiece material.
- Surface detail excellent.
- Surface roughness values in the range from 0.012 to 0.8 μm *Ra* are obtainable.
- A process capability chart showing the achievable dimensional tolerances is given opposite.

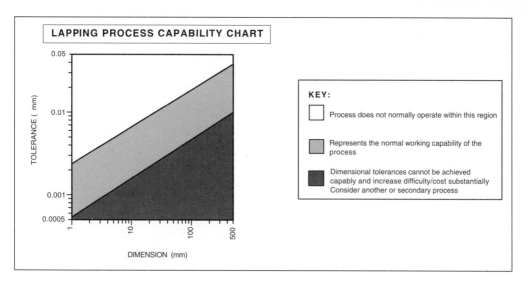

LAPPING PROCESS CAPABILITY CHART

TOLERANCE (mm)

DIMENSION (mm)

KEY:

Process does not normally operate within this region

Represents the normal working capability of the process

Dimensional tolerances cannot be achieved capably and increase difficulty/cost substantially Consider another or secondary process

5 Non-traditional machining processes

5.1 Electrical discharge machining (EDM)

Process description

- The tool, usually graphite, and the workpiece are essentially electrodes, the tool being the negative of the cavity to be produced. The workpiece is vaporized by spark discharges created by a power supply. The gap between the workpiece and tool is kept constant and a dielectric fluid is used to cool the vaporized 'chips' and then flush them away from the workpiece surface.

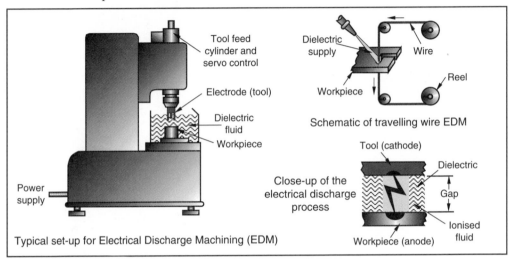

Typical set-up for Electrical Discharge Machining (EDM)

Materials

- Any electrically conductive material irrespective of material hardness, commonly, tool steels and copper alloys.
- Melting point and latent heat of melting are important properties determining the material removal rate.

Process variations

- Travelling wire EDM: wire moves slowly along the prescribed path on the workpiece and cuts the metal with sparks creating a slot of 'kerf'. CNC control is common.
- No-wear EDM: minimizing tool wear of steels by reversing the polarity and using copper tools.
- Electrical discharge grinding (EDG): graphite or brass grinding wheel rotates relative to the rotating workpiece and removes material by spark erosion (no abrasives involved).

Economic considerations

- Production rates very low.
- Material removal rates are typically 0.3 cm^3/min and is a function of the current rate.

- Lead time days to several weeks depending on complexity of electrode tool.
- Tools can be of segmented construction for high complexity work.
- Material utilization very poor. Scrap material cannot be recycled.
- High degree of automation possible.
- Economical for low production runs. Can be used for one-offs.
- Tooling costs are high.
- Equipment costs generally high.
- Direct labour costs are low to moderate.

Typical applications

- Tool and die blocks for forging, extrusions, castings, punching, blanking, etc.
- Honeycomb structures and irregular shapes.
- Prototype parts.
- Burr free parts.

Design aspects

- High degree of shape complexity possible, limited only by ability to produce tool shape.
- Travelling wire EDM limited to two-dimensional profiles.
- Suitable for small diameter, deep holes with L/D up to 20:1.
- Undercuts are possible with specialized tooling.
- Possible to machine thin and delicate sections due to minimal machining forces.
- Minimum radius = 0.025 mm.
- Minimum hole/slot size = 0.05 mm.
- Travelling wire EDM can cut sections up to 150 mm.

Quality issues

- Burr free part production.
- Produces slightly tapered holes, especially if blind, and some overcut.
- A hard skin, or recast layer, produced may offer longer life, lower friction and lubricant retention for dies, but can be removed if undesirable.
- Beneath the recast layer is a heat affected zone which may be softer than the parent material.
- Finishing cuts are made at low removal rates.
- Tool wear is related to the melting points of the materials involved and this affects accuracy. May require changing periodically.
- Being a thermal process, residual stresses and fine cracks may form.
- Removal rate can be increased with the expense of a poorer surface finish.
- Surface detail good.
- Surface roughness values are in the range from 0.05 to 12.5 μm *Ra*. Dependent on current density and material being machined.
- Achievable tolerances are in the range from ±0.005 to ±0.125 mm. (Process capability charts have not been included. Capability is not primarily driven by characteristic dimension but by the material being processed.)

5.2 Electrochemical machining (ECM)

Process description

- Workpiece material is removed by electrolysis. A tool, usually copper, (–ve electrode) of the desired shape is kept a fixed distance away from the electrically conductive workpiece (+ve electrode) which is immersed in a bath containing a fast flowing electrolyte and connected to a power supply. The workpiece is then dissolved by an electrochemical reaction to the shape of the tool. The electrolyte also removes the 'sludge' produced at the workpiece surface.

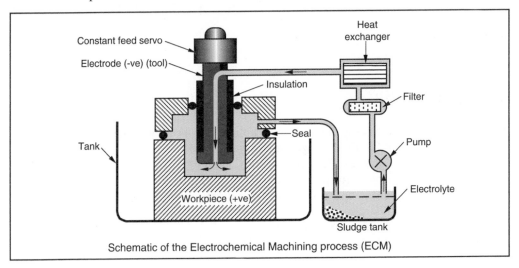

Schematic of the Electrochemical Machining process (ECM)

Materials

- Any electrically conductive material irrespective of material hardness, commonly, tool steels, nickel alloys and titanium alloys. Ceramics and copper alloys are also processed sometimes.

Process variations

- Electrochemical grinding (ECG): combination of electrochemical reaction and abrasive machining of workpiece.
- Electrochemical drilling: for the production of deep, small diameter holes.
- Electrochemical polishing, de-burring and honing.

Economic considerations

- Production rates are moderate.
- Material removal rates are typically 16 cm^3/min/1000 amp. Dependent on current density, electrolyte and gap between tool and workpiece.

- High power consumption.
- Lead time can be several weeks. Tools are very complex.
- Set-up times can be short.
- Material utilization very poor. Scrap material cannot be recycled.
- Disposal of chemicals used can be costly.
- High degree of automation possible.
- Economical for moderate to high production runs.
- Tooling costs are very high. Dedicated tooling.
- Equipment costs generally high.
- Direct labour costs are low to moderate.

Typical applications

- Hole drilling, profiling and contouring of components.
- Jet engine parts.
- Turbine blade features.
- Honeycomb structures and irregular shapes.
- Burr free parts.
- Deep holes.

Design aspects

- High degree of shape complexity possible, limited only by ability to produce tool shape.
- Suitable for small diameter, deep holes with L/D up to 50:1.
- Suitable for parts affected by thermal processes.
- Undercuts are possible with specialized tooling.
- Possible to machine thin and delicate sections due to no processing forces.
- Minimum radius = 0.05 mm.
- Minimum hole size = $\varnothing$0.1 mm.

Quality issues

- Burr-free part production.
- Produces slightly tapered holes, especially if deep, and some overcut possible.
- Finishing cuts are made at low material removal rates.
- No stresses introduced, either, thermal or mechanical.
- Virtually no tool wear.
- Arcing may cause tool damage.
- Some electrolyte solutions can be corrosive to tool, workpiece and equipment.
- Surface detail good.
- Surface roughness values are in the range from 0.2 to 6.3 µm *Ra*. Dependent on current density and material being machined.
- Achievable tolerances are in the range from ±0.01 to ±0.25 mm. (Process capability charts have not been included. Capability is not primarily driven by characteristic dimension but by the material being processed.)

5.3 Electron beam machining (EBM)

Process description

- An electron gun bombards the workpiece (which is in a vacuum chamber) with electrons up to 80% the speed of light generating localized heat and evaporating the workpiece surface. Magnetic lenses focus the electron beam and electromagnetic coils control its position.

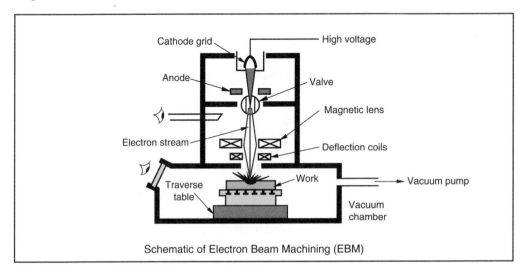

Schematic of Electron Beam Machining (EBM)

Materials

- Any material regardless of its type, electrical conductivity and hardness.

Process variations

- High-vacuum, semi-vacuum and atmospheric machines available, with the former being the most common.
- Electron beam welding (EBW): used to weld very thin sheets to thick plates with small weld area and heat affected zone and no flux or shielding.
- Electron beam processing can also be used for cutting and surface hardening.

Economic considerations

- Production rates are dependent on size of vacuum chamber and by the ability to process a number of parts in batches at each loading cycle.
- Parts should closely match size of chamber.
- Material removal rates are low, typically 2 mm^3/min.
- Lead time can be several weeks.

- Set-up times can be short, but the time to create a vacuum in the chamber at each loading cycle is an important consideration.
- Material utilization is good.
- High degree of automation possible.
- Economical for low to moderate production runs. Economical for thin parts requiring small cuts.
- Tooling costs are very high.
- Equipment costs are very high.
- Direct labour costs are high. Skilled labour required.

Typical applications

- Multiple small diameter holes in very thin and thick materials.
- Injector nozzle holes.
- Small extrusion die holes.
- Irregular shaped holes and slots.
- Engraving.
- Features in silicon wafers for the electronics industry.

Design aspects

- Electron beam path can be programmed to produce and desired pattern.
- Suitable for small diameter, deep holes with L/D up to 100:1.
- Possible to machine thin and delicate sections due to no mechanical processing forces.
- Sharp corners are difficult to produce.
- Better to have more small holes requiring less heat than a few large holes requiring considerable heat.
- Maximum thickness = 150 mm.
- Minimum hole size = ∅0.01 mm.

Quality issues

- Integrity of vacuum important. Beam dispersion occurs due to electron collision with air molecules.
- The reflectivity of the workpiece surface is important. Dull and unpolished surfaces are preferred.
- Hazardous X-rays are produced during processing which require lead shielding.
- Produces slightly tapered holes, especially if deep holes are required.
- Localized thermal stresses, heat affected zones, recast layers and distortion of thin parts may be produced. Recast layers can be removed if undesirable.
- Surface roughness values are in the range from 0.4 to 6.3 mm *Ra*.
- Achievable tolerances are in the range from ±0.01 to ±0.125 mm. (Process capability charts have not been included. Capability is not primarily driven by characteristic dimension.)

5.4 Laser beam machining (LBM)

Process description

- A pulsed beam of coherent monochromatic light of high-power density (or LASER) is focused on to the workpiece surface causing it locally to vaporize. The material then leaves the surface in the vaporized or liquid state at high velocity.

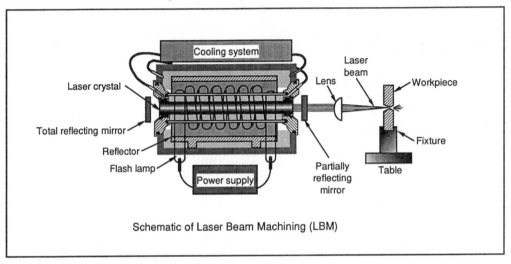

Schematic of Laser Beam Machining (LBM)

Materials

- Any material regardless of its type, electrical conductivity and hardness.

Process variations

- Laser beam machines can also be used for cutting, surface hardening, welding (LBW), drilling, blanking, engraving and trimming, by varying the power density.
- Many types of laser are available, used for different applications/material combinations. Common lasers used include: pulsed and continuous wave CO_2, Nd:YAG, Nd:glass, ruby and excimer.
- High-pressure gas streams are used to enhance the process by aiding the exothermic reaction process, keep the surrounding material cool and blowing the vaporized or molten material and slag away from the workpiece surface.

Economic considerations

- Production rates are moderate.
- Material removal rates are typically 5 mm^3/min and cutting speeds 4 m/min.
- High power consumption.
- Lead time can be short, typically weeks.
- Set-up times are short.
- Material utilization is good.

- High degree of automation possible. Integration with CNC punching machines is popular giving greater design freedom.
- Economical for low to moderate production runs.
- Tooling costs are very high.
- Equipment costs are very high.
- Direct labour costs are medium to high. Some skilled labour required.

Typical applications

- Multiple holes in very thin and thick materials.
- Non-standard shaped holes and slots.
- Prototype parts.
- Trimming, scribing and engraving of hard materials.
- Small diameter lubrication holes.
- Features in silicon wafers in the electronics industry.

Design aspects

- Laser can be directed, shaped and focused by reflective optics permitting high spatial freedom in two-dimensions.
- Suitable for small diameter, deep holes with L/D up to 50:1.
- Special techniques are required to drill blind holes.
- Possible to machine thin and delicate sections due to no mechanical contact.
- Minimal work holding fixtures are required.
- Sharp corners are possible, but radii should be provided for in the design.
- Maximum thicknesses: mild steel = 25 mm, stainless steel = 13 mm, aluminium = 10 mm.
- Maximum hole size (not profiled) = 12 mm.
- Minimum hole size = $\varnothing$0.005 mm.

Quality issues

- Difficulty of material processing is dictated by how close the material's boiling and vaporization points are.
- Localized thermal stresses, heat affected zones, recast layers and distortion of very thin parts may be produced. Recast layers can be removed if undesirable.
- The cutting of flammable materials is usually inert gas assisted. Metals are usually oxygen assisted.
- Control of the pulse duration is important to minimize the heat affected zone depth and size of molten metal pool surrounding the cut.
- The reflectivity of the workpiece surface is important. Dull and unpolished surfaces are preferred.
- Hole wall geometry can be irregular.
- Surface detail fair.
- Surface roughness values are in the range from 0.4 to 6.3 μm *Ra*.
- Achievable tolerances are in the range from ±0.015 to ±0.125 mm. (Process capability charts have not been included. Capability is not primarily driven by characteristic dimension.)

5.5 Chemical machining (CM)

Process description

- Selective chemical dissolution of the workpiece material by immersion in a bath containing an etchant (usually acid or alkali solutions). The areas that are not required to be etched are masked with 'cut and peel' tapes, paints or polymeric materials.

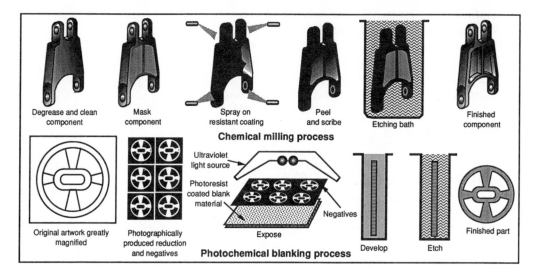

Degrease and clean component — Mask component — Spray on resistant coating — Peel and scribe — Etching bath — Finished component

Chemical milling process

Original artwork greatly magnified — Photographically produced reduction and negatives — Ultraviolet light source — Photoresist coated blank material — Negatives — Expose — Develop — Etch — Finished part

Photochemical blanking process

Materials

- Most materials can be chemically machined with the correct chemical etchant selection, commonly: ferrous, nickel, titanium, magnesium and copper alloys, and silicon.

Process variations

- Chemical milling: removal of material to a specified depth on large areas (similar to conventional milling except chemicals are used).
- Chemical blanking: used for thin parts requiring penetration through thickness.
- Photochemical blanking: uses photographic techniques to blank very thin sheets of metal, primarily for the production of printed circuit boards.
- Chemical jet machining: uses a single jet of etchant.
- Thermochemical machining: uses a hot corrosive gas.

Economic considerations

- Production rates are low to moderate. Can be improved by machining a large sheet before cutting out the individual parts. Parts can also be etched on both sides simultaneously.

- Speed of penetration is typically from 0.0025 to 0.1 mm/min but dependent on material.
- Lead times are short.
- Set-up times are short.
- Material utilization poor. Scrap material cannot be recycled.
- Disposal of chemicals used can be costly.
- Economical for low production runs. Least economical quantity is one.
- Tooling costs are low.
- Equipment costs generally low.
- Direct labour costs are low.

Typical applications

- Primarily used for weight reduction in aerospace components, panels, extrusions and forgings by producing shallow cavities.
- Printed circuit boards and features in silicon wafers for the electronics industry.
- Decorative panels and printing plates.
- Honeycomb structures, irregular contours and stepped cavities.
- Burr-free parts.

Design aspects

- High degree of shape complexity possible in two-dimensions.
- Suitable for parts affected by thermal processes.
- Undercuts are always present. The etch factor for a material is the ratio of the etched depth to the size of undercut.
- Controlling the size of small holes in thin sheet is difficult.
- Compensation for the undercut should be taken into account when designing the masking template.
- Inside edges are always radiused while outside edges have sharp corners.
- Possible to machine thin and delicate sections due to no processing forces.
- Minimum thickness = 0.013 mm.
- Maximum depth of cut = 13 mm.
- Maximum size = 3.7 m × 15 m, but dependent on bath size.

Quality issues

- Residual stresses in the part should be removed before processing to prevent distortion.
- Surfaces need to be clean and free from grease and scale to allow good masking adhesion and uniform material removal.
- Masking material should not react with the chemical etchant.
- Parts should be washed thoroughly after processing to prevent further chemical reactions.
- Porosity in castings/welds and intergranular defects are preferentially attacked by the etchant. This causes surface irregularities and non-uniformities.
- Room temperature and humidity, bath temperature and stirring need to be controlled to obtain uniform material removal.

- Surface detail is good.
- Surface roughness values are in the range from 0.2 to 6.3 mm *Ra* and are dependent on the material being processed.
- Achievable dimensional tolerances for selected process and material combinations are shown below.

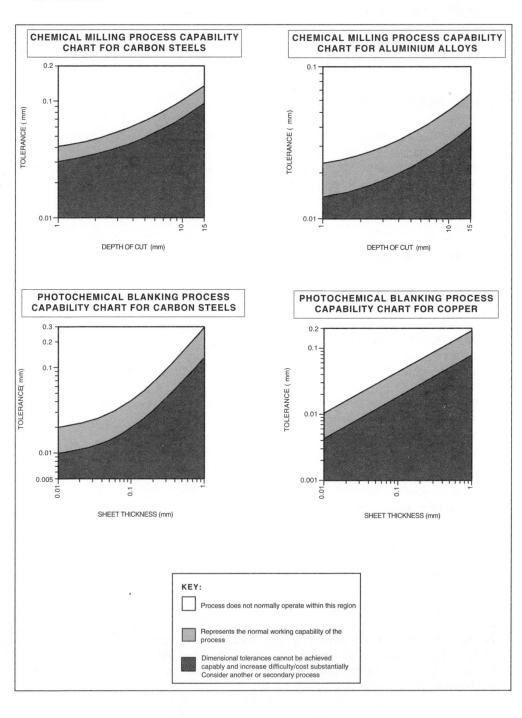

5.6   Ultrasonic machining (USM)

Process description

- The tool, which is negative of the workpiece, is vibrated at around 20 kHz with an amplitude of between 0.013 and 0.08 mm in an abrasive grit slurry at the workpiece surface. The workpiece material is removed by essentially three mechanisms: hammering of the grit against the surface by the tool, impact of free abrasive grit particles and cavitation. The slurry also removes debris away from the surface. The tool is gradually moved down maintaining a constant gap of approximately 0.1 mm between the tool and workpiece surface.

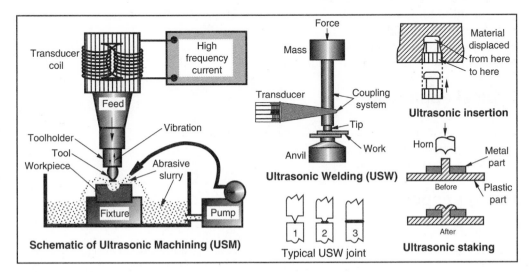

Schematic of Ultrasonic Machining (USM)

Ultrasonic Welding (USW)

Typical USW joint

Ultrasonic insertion

Ultrasonic staking

Materials

- Any material, however, brittle hard materials are preferred to ductile, for example, ceramics, precious stones, tool steels, titanium and glass.

Process variations

- Vibrations are either piezo-electric or magnetostrictive transducer generated.
- Tool materials vary with application and allowable tool wear during machining. Common tool materials are: mild steel, stainless steel, tool steel, brass and carbides.
- Abrasive grit available in many grades and material types. Materials commonly used are: boron carbide, aluminium oxide and silicon carbide.
- Rotary ultrasonic machining: uses a vibrating and rotating diamond tool, but with no abrasives.
- Ultrasonic welding (USW): uses ultrasonic vibrations to impart shearing stresses in the materials to be joined which cause local plastic deformation and eventually solid-state bonding. Used for joining sheet metal and plastic and for staking and metal inserting of plastic parts.

- Ultrasonic cleaning: uses high frequency sound waves in a liquid causing cavitation which cleans the surface of the component, similar to a scrubbing action. Used to remove scale, rust, etc.

Economic considerations

- Production rates very low.
- Material removal rates are typically 0.8 cm^3/min.
- Lead time typically days depending on complexity of tool. Special tooling required for each job.
- Material utilization poor. Scrap material cannot be recycled.
- High degree of automation possible.
- Economical for low production runs. Can be used for one-offs.
- Tooling costs are high.
- Equipment costs are generally moderate.
- Direct labour costs are low to moderate.

Typical applications

- Holes, slots and complex cavities in hard, brittle materials.
- Coining operations.
- USW common in assembly.

Design aspects

- Limited to shape of tool and control in two-dimensions.
- Avoid sharp profiles, corners and radii as abrasive slurry erodes them away.
- Overcut will be produced which is approximately twice the grit size.
- Suitable for small diameter holes with L/D up to 3:1.
- Maximum hole size = 90 mm.
- Minimum hole size = 0.08 mm.

Quality issues

- Tapering of slots and holes occurs.
- Through holes in brittle materials should have a backing plate.
- Amplitude and frequency of vibration, tool material, impact force, abrasive grit grade and slurry concentration all impact on accuracy and surface roughness.
- Finishing cuts are made at lower material removal rates.
- Difference in wear rate between the tool and workpiece materials should be as high as possible.
- Surface detail is good.
- Surface roughness values are in the range from 0.2 to 1.6 µm Ra.
- Finer surface roughness values are obtained with finer grit grades.
- Achievable tolerances are in the range from ±0.005 to ±0.05 mm. (Process capability charts have not been included. Capability is not primarily driven by characteristic dimension.)

6 Fabrication and joining processes

6.1   Tungsten inert-gas welding (TIG)

Process description

- An electric arc is automatically generated between the workpiece and a non-consumable tungsten electrode at the joint area. The parent metal is melted and the weld created with or without the addition of a filler rod. The weld area is shielded with a stable stream of inert gas, usually argon, top prevent oxidation and contamination.

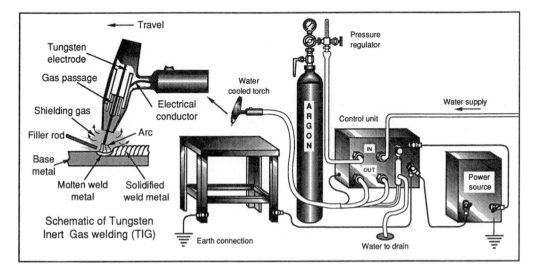

Schematic of Tungsten Inert Gas welding (TIG)

Materials

- Most non-ferrous metals (except zinc), commonly, aluminium, nickel, magnesium and titanium alloys, copper and stainless steel. Carbon steels, low alloy steels and refractory alloys can also be welded. Dissimilar metals are difficult to weld.

Process variations

- Portable manual or automated a.c. or d.c. systems: a.c. commonly used for welding aluminium and magnesium alloys.
- Pulsed TIG: excellent for thin sheet or parts with dissimilar thickness (low heat input).
- TIG spot welding: used on lap joints in thin sheets.
- Pure helium or more commonly, a helium/argon mix is used as the shielding gas for metals with high thermal conductivity, for example, copper, or material thickness >6 mm giving increased weld rates and penetration.

Economic considerations

- Weld rates vary from 0.2 m/min for manual welding to 1.5 m/min for automated systems.

- Automation is suited to long lengths of continuous weld in the same plane.
- Automation is relatively inexpensive if no filler is required, i.e. use of close fitting parts.
- Process is suited to sheet thickness less than 4 mm, heavier gauges become more expensive due to argon cost and decreased production rate. Helium/argon gas expensive but may be viable due to increased production rate.
- Economical for low production runs. Can be used for one-offs.
- Tooling costs are low to moderate.
- Equipment costs are moderate.
- Direct labour costs are moderate to high. Highly skilled labour required for manual welding. Set-up costs can be high for fabrications using automated welding.
- Finishing costs are low to moderate. There is no slag produced at the weld area, however, some grinding back of the weld may be required.

Typical applications

- Chemical plant pipe work.
- Nuclear plant fabrications.
- Aerospace structures.

Design aspects

- Design complexity is high.
- Typical joint designs possible using TIG are: butt, lap, fillet and edge. See Figure 2.2 – weld joint design, page 173.
- Design joints using minimum amount of weld, i.e. intermittent runs and simple or straight contours, although TIG is suited to automated contour following.
- Access to weld area important. Wherever possible horizontal welding should be designed for, however, TIG welding is suited to most welding positions.
- Sufficient edge distances should be designed for. Avoid welds meeting at end of runs.
- Balance the welds around the fabrication's neutral axis.
- Provision for the escape of gases and vapours in the design is important.
- Distortion in welded parts can be reduced by designing symmetry into weld lines.
- The fabrication sequence should be examined with respect to the above.
- Minimum sheet thickness = 0.1 mm.
- Maximum sheet thickness, commonly:
  - copper and refractory alloys = 3 mm
  - 54carbon, low alloy and stainless steels; magnesium and nickel alloys = 6 mm aluminium and titanium alloys = 15 mm.
- Multiple weld runs required on sheet thickness ≥ 4 mm.
- Unequal thicknesses are possible.

Quality issues

- Clean, high quality welds with low distortion can be produced.
- Access for weld inspection important.
- Joint edge and surface preparation is important. Contaminates must be removed from the weld area to avoid porosity and inclusions.

- A heat affected zone always present. Some stress relieving may be required for restoration of materials original physical properties.
- Not recommended for site work in wind where the shielding gas may be gusted.
- Control of arc length is important for uniform weld properties and penetration.
- Need for jigs and fixtures to keep joints rigid during welding and subsequent cooling to reduce distortion on large fabrications.
- Selection of correct filler rod is important (where required).
- Care is needed to keep filler rod within the shielding gas to prevent oxidation.
- Workpiece and filler rod must be away from the tungsten electrode to prevent contamination which can cause an unstable arc.
- The shielding gas must be kept on for a second or two to allow tungsten electrode to cool and prevent oxidation.
- Welding variables should be preset and controlled during production.
- Automation reduces the ability to weld mating parts with inherent size and shape variations, however, it does reduce distortion, improve reproduction and produces fewer welding defects.
- 'Weldability' of the material is important and combines many of the basic properties that govern the ease with which a material can be welded and the quality of the finished weld, i.e. porosity and cracking. Material composition (alloying elements, grain structure and impurities) and physical properties (thermal conductivity, specific heat and thermal expansion) are some important attributes which determine weldability.
- Surface finish of weld is excellent.
- Fabrication tolerances are typically ±0.5 mm.

6.2 Metal inert-gas welding (MIG)

Process description

- An electric arc is manually created between the workpiece and a consumable wire electrode at the joint area. The parent metal is melted and the weld created with the continuous feed of the wire which acts as the filler metal. The weld area is shielded with a stable stream of argon or CO_2 to prevent oxidation and contamination.

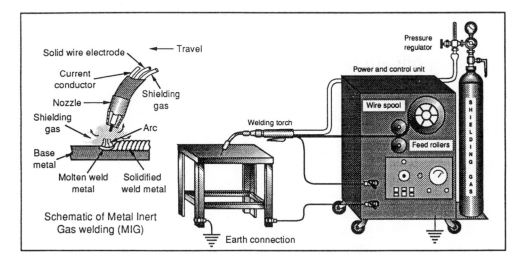

Solid wire electrode
Travel
Current conductor
Nozzle
Shielding gas
Shielding gas
Arc
Base metal
Molten weld metal
Solidified weld metal

Schematic of Metal Inert Gas welding (MIG)

Pressure regulator
Power and control unit
Wire spool
Welding torch
Feed rollers
SHIELDING GAS

Earth connection

Materials

- Carbon, low alloy and stainless steels. Most non-ferrous metals (except zinc) are also weldable; aluminium, nickel, magnesium and titanium alloys and copper. Refractory alloys and cast iron can also be welded. Dissimilar metals are difficult to weld.

Process variations

- Portable semi-automatic (manually operated) or fully automated d.c. systems and robot mounted.
- Three types of metal transfer to the weld area: dip and pulsed transfer use low current for positional welding (vertical, overhead) and thin sheet; spray transfer uses high currents for thick sheet and high deposition rates, typically for horizontal welding.
- Shielding gases: pure CO_2 or argon/CO_2 mix commonly used for carbon and low alloy steels, or a mix of argon/helium which is also used for nickel alloys and copper. Pure argon is used for aluminium alloys. High chromium steels use an argon/O_2 mix.
- MIG spot welding: used on lap joints.
- Flux cored arc welding (FCAW): uses a wire containing a flux and gas generating compounds for self-shielding, although flux cored wire is preferred with additional shielding gas for certain conditions.

Economic considerations

- Weld rates up to 0.5 m/min for manual welding.
- High weld deposition rates with continuous operation reduce production costs.
- Well suited to traversing automated and robotic systems.
- Choice of electrode wire ($\varnothing$0.5–1.5 mm) and shielding gas are important cost considerations.
- Economical for low production runs. Can be used for one-offs.
- Tooling costs are low to moderate. Equipment costs are moderate.
- Direct labour costs are low to moderate to high. Skill level required is less than TIG.
- Finishing costs are low to moderate. There is no slag produced at the weld area, however, some grinding back of the weld may be required.

Typical applications

- General fabrication.
- Structural steelwork.
- Automobile bodywork.

Design aspects

- All levels of complexity possible.
- Typical joint designs possible using MIG are: butt, lap, fillet and edge. MIG excellent for vertical and overhead welding. See Figure 2.2 – weld joint design, page 171.
- Design joints using minimum amount of weld, i.e. intermittent runs.
- Welds should be designed with simple or straight contours.
- Balance the welds around the fabrication's neutral axis.
- Access to weld area important. MIG good for welds inaccessible by other methods.
- Sufficient edge distances should be designed for and avoid welds meeting at the end of runs.
- Provision for the escape of gases and vapours in the design is important.
- Distortion in welded parts can be reduced by designing symmetry into weld lines.
- The fabrication sequence should be examined with respect to the above.
- Minimum sheet thickness = 0.5 mm (6 mm for cast iron).
- Maximum sheet thickness, commonly:
  refractory alloys = 6 mm
  carbon, low alloy and stainless steels; cast iron, aluminium, magnesium, nickel, titanium alloys and copper = 80 mm.
- Multiple weld runs required on sheet thicknesses $\geq$ 6 mm.
- Unequal thicknesses are possible.

Quality issues

- Clean, high quality welds with low distortion can be produced.
- Access for weld inspection important.
- Joint edge and surface preparation is important. Contaminates must be removed from the weld area to avoid porosity and inclusions.

- Shielding gas is chosen to suit parent metal, i.e. it must not react when welding.
- Wire electrode must closely match the composition of the metals being welded.
- The slag created when using a flux cored wire may aid the control of the weld profile and is commonly used for site work (windy conditions where the shielding gas may be gusted or positional welding) and large fillet welds.
- A heat affected zone always present. Some stress relieving may be required for restoration of materials original physical properties.
- Cracking may be experienced when welding high alloy steels.
- Self-adjusting arc length reduces skill level required and increases weld uniformity.
- Need for jigs and fixtures to keep joints rigid during welding and subsequent cooling to reduce distortion on large fabrications.
- Welding variables should be preset and controlled during production.
- Automation can limit the ability to weld mating parts with large size and shape variations, however, the use of dedicated tooling does reduce distortion, improve reproduction and produces fewer welding defects.
- 'Weldability' of the material is important and combines many of the basic properties that govern the ease with which a material can be welded and the quality of the finished weld, i.e. porosity and cracking. Material composition (alloying elements, grain structure and impurities) and physical properties (thermal conductivity, specific heat and thermal expansion) are some important attributes which determine weldability.
- Surface finish of weld is good.
- Fabrication tolerances are typically ±0.5 mm.

6.3   Manual metal arc welding (MMA)

Process description

- An electric arc is created between a consumable electrode and the workpiece at the joint area. The parent metal is melted and the weld created with the manual feed of the electrode along the weld line and downwards as the electrode is being consumed. Simultaneously, a flux on the outside of the electrode melts covering the weld pool and generates a gas shielding it from the atmosphere.

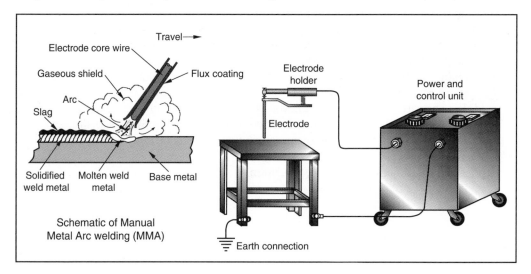

Materials

- Carbon, low alloy and stainless steels; nickel alloys and cast iron. Welding of non-ferrous metals is not recommended. Dissimilar metals are difficult to weld.

Process variations

- Manual d.c. and a.c. sets. Only a few fluxes give stable operation with a.c.
- Large selection of electrodes materials with a variety of flux types for the welding of different metals and properties required. Core sizes are between $\emptyset$1.6 and 9.5 mm and the electrode length is usually 460 mm.

Economic considerations

- Weld rates up to 0.2 m/min.
- Most flexible of all welding processes.
- Can weld a variety of metals by simply changing the electrode.
- a.c. welding requires more power than d.c.

- Suitable for site work. Welding can be performed up to 20 m away from power supply.
- Non-continuous process. Frequent changes of electrode are required.
- Economical for low production runs. Can be used for one-offs.
- Tooling costs are low. Need for jigs and fixtures not as important as other methods and less accuracy required in setting-up.
- Equipment costs are low.
- Direct labour costs are high. Skill level required is higher than MIG.
- Finishing costs are moderate to high. Slag produced at the weld area which must be removed during runs and some grinding back of the weld may be required.

Typical applications

- Pressure vessels.
- Structural steelwork.
- Pipework.
- Machine plant.
- Maintenance.

Design aspects

- All levels of complexity possible.
- Typical joint designs possible using MMA are: butt, lap, fillet and edge in heavier sections. See Figure 2.2 – weld joint design, page 171.
- Suitable for all welding positions.
- Design joints using minimum amount of weld, i.e. intermittent runs.
- Balance the welds around the fabrication's neutral axis.
- Welds should be designed with simple or straight contours.
- Access to weld area important. MMA excellent for welds inaccessible by other methods.
- Sufficient edge distances should be designed for. Avoid welds meeting at end of runs.
- Provision for the escape of gases and vapours in the design is important.
- Distortion in welded parts can be reduced by designing symmetry into weld lines.
- The fabrication sequence should be examined with respect to the above.
- Minimum sheet thickness = 1.5 mm (6 mm for cast iron).
- Maximum sheet thickness, commonly for carbon, low alloy and stainless steels, nickel alloys and cast iron = 200 mm.
- Multiple weld runs required on sheet thicknesses ≥ 10 mm.
- Unequal thicknesses are difficult.

Quality issues

- Moderate to high quality welds with acceptable levels of distortion can be produced.
- Quality and consistency of weld is related to skill of welder to maintain correct arc length and burn-off rate.
- Access for weld inspection important.
- Joint edge and surface preparation is important. Contaminates must be removed from the weld area to avoid porosity and inclusions.

- A heat affected zone always present. Some stress relieving may be required for restoration of materials original physical properties.
- Can alter composition of weld by addition of alloying elements in the electrode. Addition of deoxidants in the flux minimizes carbon loss, which reduces weld strength.
- Electrodes must be dry and free from oil and grease to prevent weld contamination.
- Low hydrogen electrodes should be used when welding high carbon steels to reduce chance of hydrogen cracking.
- The protective slag can help the weld to keep its shape during positional welding.
- Weld is ideally left to cool to room temperature before the slag is removed.
- When the electrode's length is reduced to approximately 50 mm it should be replaced.
- Welding current should be maintained during welding with a stable power supply.
- Arc deflection can sometimes occur with d.c. supplies, especially in magnetized metals. The workpiece may need demagnetizing or the return cable repositioned.
- Pre-heating of workpiece can reduce porosity and hydrogen cracking.
- 'Weldability' of the material is important and combines many of the basic properties that govern the ease with which a material can be welded and the quality of the finished weld, i.e. porosity and cracking. Material composition (alloying elements, grain structure and impurities) and physical properties (thermal conductivity, specific heat and thermal expansion) are some important attributes which determine weldability.
- Surface finish of weld is fair to good.
- Fabrication tolerances are typically ±1 mm.

6.4   Submerged arc welding (SAW)

Process description

- A blanket of flux is fed from a hopper in advance of an electric arc created between a consumable electrode wire and the workpiece at the joint area. The arc melts the parent metal and the wire creates the weld as it is automatically fed downwards and traversed along the weld line or the work is moved under welding head. The flux shields the weld pool from the atmosphere and any flux that is not used is recycled.

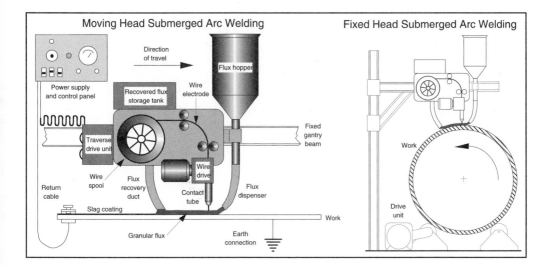

Materials

- Carbon, low alloy and stainless steels, and some nickel alloys. Dissimilar metals are difficult to weld, however, hardfacing can be performed using flat electrode wire.

Process variations

- Self-contained, mainly automated a.c. or d.c systems with up to three welding heads.
- Can have manual traversing on wheels (ship's deck plates) or self-propelled traversing on a gantry (moving head types) and fixed head where the work rotates (pressure vessels).
- Copper coated electrode wire can be solid or tubular. Tubular is used to supply the weld with additional alloying elements. Wire sizes range from ∅0.8 to 9.5 mm.
- Fluxes available in powdered or granulated form, either neutral or basic. Neutral fluxes used for low carbon steel and basic fluxes for higher carbon steels.
- Bulk welding: uses an iron powder placed in the joint gap in advance of the flux and electrode to increase deposition rates.

Economic considerations

- Highest weld deposition rate of all arc welding processes, up to 5 m/min.
- Economic for straight, continuous welds on thick plate using single or multiple runs.
- High power consumption offset by high productivity.
- Economical for low production runs. Can be used for one-offs.
- Tooling costs are low to moderate. Need for jigs and fixtures important for accurate joint alignment.
- Equipment costs are moderate to high.
- Direct labour costs are moderate. Skill level required is low to moderate, but flux handling costs can be high.
- Finishing costs are moderate to high. Slag produced at the weld area needs to be removed.

Typical applications

- Ships.
- Bridges.
- Pressure vessels.
- Structural steelwork.
- Pipework.

Design aspects

- Design complexity is limited.
- Typical joint designs possible using SAW are butt and fillet in heavier sections. See Figure 2.2 – weld joint design, page 171.
- Suitable for horizontal welding, but can perform vertical welding with special copper side plates to retain flux and mould the weld pool.
- Welds should be designed with straight runs.
- Minimum sheet thickness = 5 mm (6 mm for nickel alloys).
- Maximum sheet thickness, commonly:
  carbon, low alloy and stainless steels = 300 mm
  nickel alloys = 20 mm.
- Multiple weld runs required on sheet thicknesses ≥ 40 mm.
- Unequal thicknesses are very difficult.

Quality issues

- High quality welds can be produced with low levels of distortion due to fast welding rates.
- Good weld uniformity and properties, although on large deposit welds a coarse grain structure is formed giving inferior weld toughness.
- Access for weld inspection important.
- Large weld beads can cause cracking. Weld penetration can be controlled by using a backing strip when using high currents.

- Joint edge and surface preparation is important. Contaminates must be removed from the weld area to avoid porosity and inclusions.
- A heat affected zone always present. Some stress relieving may be required for restoration of materials original physical properties.
- Can alter composition of weld by addition of alloying elements in the electrode.
- Flux must be clean and free from moisture to prevent weld contamination.
- Weld is ideally left to cool to room temperature to allow the slag to peel off.
- Welding variables are automatically controlled. Monitoring of welding voltage is used to control arc length through varying the wire feed rate improving weld quality.
- Pre-heating of workpiece can reduce porosity and hydrogen cracking, especially on high carbon steels.
- 'Weldability' of the material is important and combines many of the basic properties that govern the ease with which a material can be welded and the quality of the finished weld, i.e. porosity and cracking. Material composition (alloying elements, grain structure and impurities) and physical properties (thermal conductivity, specific heat and thermal expansion) are some important attributes which determine weldability.
- Surface finish of weld is good.
- Fabrication tolerances are typically ±2 mm.

6.5 Resistance welding

Process description

- Resistance in the material to a timed flow of electric current at the contacting surfaces of the two parts to be joined generates heat locally, fusing them together and creating the weld with the addition of pressure provided by two current supplying electrodes or platens.

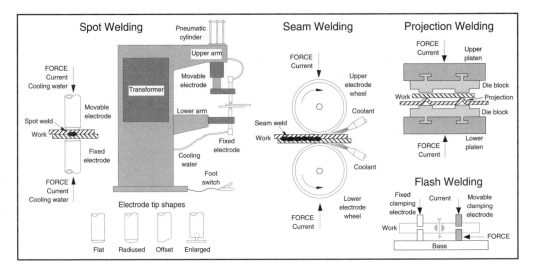

Materials

- Low carbon steels commonly, however, almost any material combination can be welded. Not recommended for cast iron, low melting point metals and high carbon steels.

Process variations

- Spot welding: uses two water cooled copper alloy electrodes of various forms. Can be manual portable (gun), single or multi-spot semi-automatic or automatic floor standing (rocker arm or press) or robot mounted as an end effector.
- Seam welding: uses two driven copper alloy wheels. Current is supplied in rapid pulses creating a series of overlapping spot welds which is pressure tight. Usually floor standing equipment, either circular, longitudinal or universal types.
- Projection welding: a component and sheet metal are clamped between platens. Localized welding takes place at the projections on the component at the contact area. Usually floor standing equipment, either single or multi-projection press type.
- Flash welding: parts are accurately aligned at their ends and clamped by the electrodes. The current is applied and the ends brought together removing the high spots at the contact area deoxidizing the joint (known as flashing). Second part is the application of pressure effectively forging the weld.

Economic considerations

- Full automation and integration with component assembly is relatively easy.
- High production rates possible due to short weld times.
- No filler metals or fluxes required.
- Little or no post-welding heat treatment is required.
- Economical for low production runs. Can be used for one-offs.
- Tooling costs are low to moderate.
- Equipment costs are moderate to high.
- Direct labour costs are low. Skill operators are not required.
- Finishing costs are very low. Hardly any finishing required.

Typical applications

- Spot welding: automobile bodies, aircraft structures, light structural fabrications and domestic appliances.
- Seam welding: fuel tanks, cans and radiators.
- Projection welding: bushes, nuts, pins, studs and screws to sheet metal. Wire mesh.
- Flash welding: railway lines, chain links, bars, tubes and tool cutting tips.

Design aspects

- Typical joint designs are: lap (spot and seam welding), edge (seam welding), butt (flash welding) and attachments (projection welding).
- Access to weld area is important.
- Can be used for joints inaccessible by other methods or where welded components are closely situated.
- Can process some coated sheet metals.
- Same end cross sections are required for flash welding.
- For spot, seam and projection welding:
  - minimum sheet thickness = 0.3 mm
  - maximum sheet thickness, commonly = 6 mm
  - (mild steel sheet up to 20 mm thick has been spot and seam welded but requires high currents and expensive equipment).
- For flash welding, sizes range from 0.2 mm thick sheet to sections up to 0.1 m^2 in area.
- Unequal thicknesses are possible with spot and seam welding (up to 3:1 thickness ratio).

Quality issues

- Clean, high quality welds with low distortion can be produced due to localized processing.
- Small heat affected zone always created.
- Surface preparation is important to remove any contaminates from the weld area such as oxide layers, paint and thick films of grease and oil. Resistance welding of aluminium requires special surface preparation.

- Welding variables should be preset and controlled during production, these include: current, timing and pressure.
- Electrodes or platens must efficiently transfer pressure to the weld, conduct and concentrate the current and remove heat away from the weld area, therefore, maintenance should be performed at regular intervals.
- Spot, seam and projection welds can be difficult to inspect. Destructive testing should be intermittently performed to monitor weld quality.
- Alignment of parts to give good contact at the joint area is important for consistent weld quality.
- Depression left behind in spot and seam welding serves to prevent cavities or cracks due to contraction of the cooling metal.
- Possibility of galvanic corrosion when resistance welding some dissimilar metals.
- High strength welds are produced by flash welding. Always leaves a ridge at the joint area which must be removed.
- 'Weldability' of the material is important and combines many of the basic properties that govern the ease with which a material can be welded and the quality of the finished weld, i.e. porosity and cracking. Material composition (alloying elements, grain structure and impurities) and physical properties (thermal conductivity, specific heat and thermal expansion) are some important attributes which determine weldability.
- Surface finish of the welds is fair to good.
- Repeatability is typically ±0.5 to ±1 mm for robot spot welding. Alignment tolerances for flash welding are between 0.1 and 0.25 mm total.

6.6 Gas welding

Process description

- High-pressure gaseous fuel and oxygen are supplied by a torch through a nozzle to the weld area where combustion takes place giving a controllable flame which melts the parent metal. Shielding from the atmosphere is performed by the outer flame. Filler metal can be supplied to the weld pool if needed.

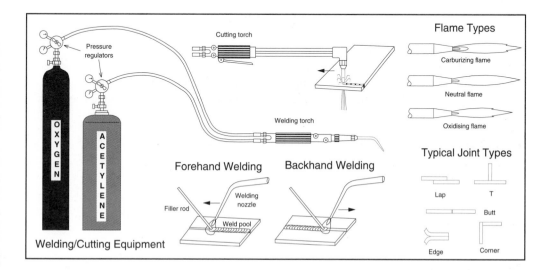

Materials

- Commonly ferrous alloys; low carbon, low alloy and stainless steels and cast iron. Nickel, copper and aluminium alloys and some low melting point metals also.

Process variations

- Commonly manually operated, portable and self-contained welding sets. Can use forehand or backhand welding procedure. Can be automated successfully.
- Gas fuel can be either: acetylene (for most welding applications and materials, known as oxyacetylene welding); hydrogen; propane, butane and natural gas are used for low temperature metals, brazing or welding small and thin parts. Air can be used instead of oxygen for brazing, soldering and welding lead sheet.
- Flux may be necessary for welding metals other than ferrous alloys.
- By regulating the oxygen flow, three types of flame can be produced: carburizing (for flame hardening, brazing, welding nickel alloys and high carbon steels), neutral (for most welding operations) and oxidizing (used for welding copper, brass and bronze).

- Pressure gas welding: heat from oxyacetylene burning is used to melt ends of the parts to be joined and then externally applied pressure welds them together.
- Gas cutting: an oxyacetylene or oxypropane flame from a specially designed nozzle is used to preheat the parent metal and an additional high pressure oxygen supply effectively cuts the metal by oxidizing it. Can perform straight cuts or profiles (when automated) in plate >500 mm thick.

Economic considerations

- Weld rates very slow, typically 0.1 m/min.
- Very flexible process. Same set can be used for welding, cutting and heat treatment.
- Economical for very low production runs. Can be used for one-offs.
- Tooling costs are low to moderate. Little tooling required and jigs and fixtures are simple for manual operation.
- Equipment costs are low to moderate.
- Direct labour costs are moderate to high. Skilled operators maybe required.
- Finishing costs are low to moderate. No slag produced, but cleaning may be required.

Typical applications

- Light fabrications in thin sheet metal.
- Ventilation ducts.
- Small diameter pipework.
- Repair work.

Design aspects

- Moderate levels of complexity possible.
- Typical joint designs possible using gas welding are: butt, fillet, lap and edge, in thin sheet (see Figure 6.6).
- Welds should be designed with simple or straight contours.
- Design joints using minimum amount of weld, i.e. intermittent runs.
- Balance the welds around the fabrication's neutral axis.
- All welding positions possible.
- Sufficient edge distances should be designed for and to avoid welds meeting at the end of runs.
- Distortion in welded parts can be reduced by designing symmetry into weld lines.
- The fabrication sequence should be examined with respect to the above.
- Minimum sheet thickness = 0.5 mm (3 mm for cast iron).
- Maximum sheet thickness, commonly:
  – carbon steel and cast iron = 30 mm
  – low alloy steel, stainless steel, nickel and aluminium alloys = 3 mm.
- Multiple weld runs required on sheet thicknesses ≥ 4 mm.
- Unequal thicknesses are possible.

Quality issues

- Good quality welds with low to moderate distortion can be produced, however, repeatability can be a problem.
- Access for weld inspection important.
- Attention to adequate jigs and fixtures when welding thin sheet is recommended to avoid excessive distortion of parts by providing good fit-up and to take heat away from the surrounding metal.
- Heat affected zone always created. Some stress relieving may be required for restoration of materials original physical properties.
- Surface preparation is important to remove any contaminates from the weld area such as oxide layers, paint and thick films of grease and oil.
- Gas flow rates should be preset and regulated during production. Gas mixes of 1:1 give the neutral flame most commonly used for welding.
- Capability to weld mating parts with large size and shape variations when under operator control of weld pool.
- Shielding integrity at the weld area not as high as arc welding methods and some oxidation and atmospheric attack may occur.
- 'Weldability' of the material is important and combines many of the basic properties that govern the ease with which a material can be welded and the quality of the finished weld, i.e. porosity and cracking. Material composition (alloying elements, grain structure and impurities) and physical properties (thermal conductivity, specific heat and thermal expansion) are some important attributes which determine weldability.
- Surface finish of weld is fair to good.
- Fabrication tolerances are typically ±1 mm.

6.7 Brazing

Process description

- Heat is applied to the parts to be joined which melts a manually fed or preplaced filler metal (which has a melting temperature $\geq 450°C$) into the joint by capillary action. A flux is usually applied to facilitate 'wetting' of the joint, prevent oxidation, remove oxides and reduce fuming.

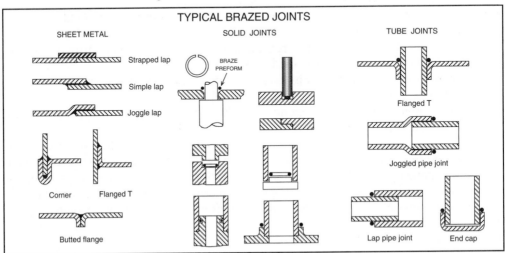

Materials

- Almost any metal and combination of metals can be brazed.

Process variations

- Gas brazing: neutral or carburizing oxy-fuel flame is used to heat the parts. Can be manual (hand-held torch) for small production runs or automated (fixed burner).
- Induction and resistance heating methods: fast, localized and uniform heating. Not recommended for brazing dissimilar metals.
- Dip brazing: parts immersed to a certain depth in molten salt-bath which is at the filler melting temperature. No flux is required.
- Furnace brazing: heating takes place in carburizing/inert atmosphere or a vacuum. The filler metal is preplaced at the joint and no additional flux is needed. Large numbers of parts of varying sizes and joint types can be brazed simultaneously. Good for parts that may distort using localized heating methods and dissimilar metals.
- Braze welding: filler metal does not flow into the joint but is built-up to create a fillet.
- Filler metal can be in preforms, wire, foil, coatings, slugs and pastes in a variety of metal alloys, commonly the alloys are based on: copper, silver, nickel and aluminium.
- Flux types: borax, borates, fluoroborates, alkali-fluorides and -chlorides (for brazing aluminium and its alloys) in powder, pastes or liquid form.

Economic considerations

- High production rates are possible. Very flexible process.
- Large fabrications may be better suited to welding than brazing.
- Economical for very low production runs. Can be used for one-offs.
- Tooling costs are low. Little tooling required.
- Equipment costs vary depending on process and degree of automation.
- Direct labour costs are low to moderate. Cost of joint preparation can be high.
- Finishing costs are moderate. Cleaning of the parts to remove flux residues is critical.

Typical applications

- Machine parts.
- Pipework and bicycle frames.
- Repair work.
- Cutting tool inserts.

Design aspects

- All levels of complexity.
- Joints should be designed to operate in shear or compression, not tension (see Figure 6.7).
- Typical joint designs possible using brazing are: lap and scarf in thin joints with large contact areas or a combination of lap and fillet. Fillets can help to distribute stresses at the joint. Butt joints are possible but can cause stress concentrators in bending.
- Lap joints should have a length to thickness ratio of between three and four times that of the thinnest part for optimum strength.
- Joints should be designed to give a clearance between the mating parts of typically, 0.02–0.2 mm depending on the process to be used and the material to be joined (can be zero for some process/material combinations). The clearance directly affects joint strength. If the clearance is too great the joint will lose a considerable amount of strength.
- A strength lying between the parent and filler metals is obtained in a well designed joint.
- Tolerances on mating parts should maintain the joint clearances recommended.
- Design joints for ease of filler metal flow, preferably with the aid of gravity. Vertical brazing should integrate chamfers on parts to create reservoirs.
- Jigs and fixtures should be used only on parts where self-locating mechanisms (staking, press fits, knurls and spot welds) are not practical. If jigs and fixtures are used they should support the joint as far from the joint area as possible, have minimum contact and have low thermal mass.
- Provision for the escape of gases and vapours in the joint design is important.
- Metals with a melting temperature less than 650°C cannot be brazed.
- Minimum sheet thickness = 0.1 mm.
- Maximum thickness = 50 mm.
- Unequal thicknesses are possible but sudden changes in section can create stress concentrators.
- Dissimilar metals can cause thermal stresses on cooling.

Quality issues

- Good quality joints with very low distortion are produced.
- Virtually a stress free joint is created with proper control of cooling.
- Choice of filler metal important in order to avoid joint embrittlement. Possibility of galvanic corrosion.
- A limited amount of interalloying takes place between the filler metal and the part metal, however, excessive alloying can reduce joint strength. Control of the time and temperature of the applied heat is important with respect to this.
- Subsequent heating of assembly after brazing could melt the filler metal again.
- Filler metal selection is based upon the metals to be brazed, process to be used and its economics, and the operating temperature of the finished assembly.
- Surface preparation is important to remove any contaminates from the joint area such as oxide layers, paint and thick films of grease and oil.
- Smooth surfaces are preferred to rough ones. Sand blasted surfaces are not recommended as they tend to reduce joint strength.
- Flux residues after the joint has been made must be removed to avoid corrosion.
- Surface finish of brazed joints is good.
- Fabrication tolerances are a function of the accuracy of the component parts and the assembly/jigging method.

6.8 Soldering

Process description

- Similar to brazing except the melting temperature of the filler metal is less than 450°C.

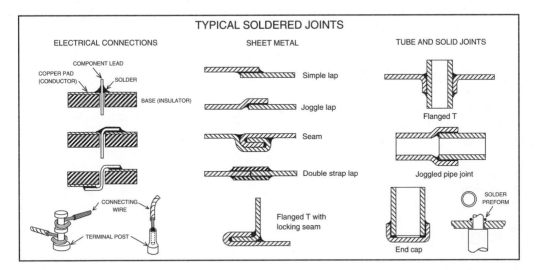

TYPICAL SOLDERED JOINTS

ELECTRICAL CONNECTIONS — SHEET METAL — TUBE AND SOLID JOINTS

COMPONENT LEAD
COPPER PAD (CONDUCTOR) SOLDER
BASE (INSULATOR)

Simple lap
Joggle lap
Seam
Double strap lap

Flanged T
Joggled pipe joint

CONNECTING WIRE
TERMINAL POST

Flanged T with locking seam

End cap

SOLDER PREFORM

Materials

- Most metals and combination of metals can be soldered with the correct selection of filler metal, heating process and flux. Commonly, copper, tin, mild and low alloy steels, nickel and precious metals are soldered. Magnesium, titanium, cast iron and high carbon/alloy steels are not recommended. Some ceramics can be soldered.

Process variations

- Flame soldering: air-fuel flame is used to heat the parts. Can be manual (hand-held torch) for small production runs or automated (fixed burner) for greater economy.
- Furnace soldering: uniform heating takes place in an inert atmosphere or vacuum.
- Induction or resistance heating methods: fast, localized and uniform heating.
- Dip soldering: parts immersed to a certain depth in a bath of molten filler metal. Includes wave soldering used extensively for electronic printed circuit board manufacture.
- Contact soldering: uses an electrically heated iron or hot plate. Most common process.
- Infra-red and vapour phase reflow soldering: provide uniform heating.
- Filler metal (solder) can be in preforms, wire, foil, coatings, slugs and pastes in a variety of metal alloys, commonly: tin-lead, tin-zinc, lead-silver, zinc-aluminium and cadmium-silver. The selection is based upon the metals to be soldered.
- Flux types: either corrosive (rosin, muriatic acid, metal chlorides) or non-corrosive (aniline phosphate), in powder, pastes or liquid form.

Economic considerations

- High production rates are possible for dip soldering.
- Very flexible process.
- Economical for very low production runs. Can be used for one-offs.
- Tooling costs are low. Little tooling required.
- Equipment costs vary depending on degree of automation.
- Direct labour costs are low to moderate. Cost of joint preparation can be high.
- Finishing costs are moderate. Cleaning of the parts to remove flux residues is critical.

Typical applications

- Electrical connections.
- Printed circuit boards.
- Pipework.
- Automobile radiators.
- Precision parts.
- Jewellery.

Design aspects

- Design complexity is high.
- Used to provide electrical or thermal conductivity or to provide pressure tight joints.
- Joints should be designed to operate in shear and not tension (see Figure 6.8). Additional mechanical fixing is recommended on highly stressed joints.
- Most common joint is the lap with large contact areas or a combination of lap and fillet. Fillet joints are predominantly used in electrical connections.
- On lap joints the length of lap should be between three and four times that of the thinnest part for optimum strength.
- Joints should be designed to give a clearance between the mating parts of 0.08–0.18 mm.
- Design joints using minimum amount of solder.
- Jigs and fixtures should be used only on parts where self-locating mechanisms, i.e. seaming, staking, knurls, bending or punch marks are not practical. If jigs and fixtures are used they should support the joint as far from the joint as possible, have minimum contact with the parts to be soldered and have low thermal mass.
- Joints are designed to avoid flow of solder against gravity. Machine marks should be in line with the flow of solder.
- Soldered joints in electronic printed circuit boards should be spaced more than 0.8 mm apart.
- Provision for the escape of gases and vapours in the design is important with vent-holes.
- Minimum sheet thickness = 0.1 mm.
- Maximum sheet thickness, commonly = 6 mm.
- Unequal thicknesses are possible but may create unequal joint expansion.
- Dissimilar metals can cause thermal stresses at the joint on cooling due to different expansion coefficients.

Quality issues

- Virtually stress and distortion free joints can be produced.
- Coating metals with tin improves solderability.
- Coatings should be used on parts to protect the parent metal prior to soldering, classed as: protective, fusible, soluble, non-soluble and stop-off coatings.
- Control of the time and temperature of the applied heat is important.
- Contamination free environment important in electronics soldering.
- Subsequent operations should have a lower processing temperature than the solder melting temperature.
- Heat sinks should be used when soldering heat-sensitive components, especially in electronics manufacture.
- Jigs and fixtures should be used to maintain joint location during solder cooling for delicate assemblies.
- Choice of solder important in order to avoid possibility of galvanic corrosion.
- Surface preparation is important to remove any contaminates from the joint area such as oxide layers, paint and thick films of grease and oil. Degreasing and pickling of the parts to be soldered is recommended.
- Smooth surfaces are preferred to rough ones.
- Flux residues after the joint has been made must be removed to avoid corrosion.
- Surface finish of soldered joints is excellent.
- Fabrication tolerances are a function of the accuracy of the component parts and the assembly/jigging method.

6.9 Adhesive bonding

Process description

- Joining of similar or dissimilar materials by the application of a natural or synthetic substances to their mating surfaces which set 'cold' or with the application of heat and/or pressure. Can replace or compliment conventional joining methods.

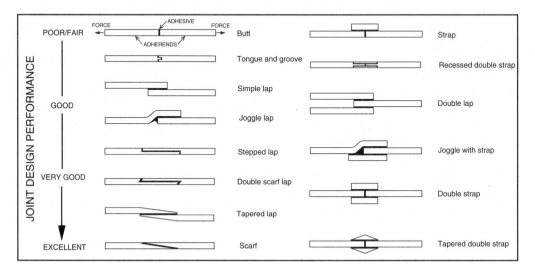

Materials

- Most materials or combination of materials can be bonded with the correct selection of adhesive, surface preparation and joint design. Problems may be encountered in bonding materials which have surface oxides, or which are plated or painted.

Process variations

- Adhesives available in many forms: liquids, pastes, tapes, powder and granules.
- Curing mechanisms can be: heat, pressure, time, chemical catalyst, vulcanization or reactivation, or a combination of these.
- Adhesives can be applied manually or automatically by: brushing, spraying or roll coating.
- Many types of adhesive are available: natural animal and vegetable glues, epoxies (typically uses a two-part resin and hardener or single part cured by heat), anaerobics (sets in the absence of atmospheric oxygen), cyanoacrylates (uses surface moisture as the hardening catalyst), hot melts (thermoplastic resin bonds as it cools), phenolics (based on phenol formaldehyde thermosetting resins, two-part cold or heat cured), plastisols (based on PVC and uses heat to cure), polyurethanes (similar to two-part epoxies), rubber adhesives (rubber compounds in a solvent which evaporates to cure), toughened adhesives (acrylic or epoxy based cured by a number of methods and can withstand high shock loads) and tapes (pressure sensitive adhesives).

Economic considerations

- High production rates are possible.
- Very flexible process. Can aid weight minimization in critical applications or where other joining methods are not suitable.
- Simplifies the assembly process and therefore can reduce costs.
- Economical for low production runs. Can be used for one-offs.
- Tooling costs are low to medium. Jigs and fixtures recommended during curing procedure.
- Equipment costs are generally low.
- Direct labour costs are low to moderate. Cost of joint preparation can be high.
- Finishing costs are low. Little or no finishing required.

Typical applications

- Building and structural applications.
- Automotive, marine and aerospace assemblies.
- Packaging and stationary.
- Furniture and footwear.

Design aspects

- All levels of complexity.
- Joints should be designed to operate in shear, not tension (see Figure 6.9). Adhesives have relatively low strength and additional mechanical fixing is recommended on highly stressed joints to avoid peeling.
- Most common joint is the lap or variations on the lap, for example, the tapered lap and scarf (preferred). Can also incorporate straps and self-locating mechanisms. Butt joints are not recommended on thin sections.
- A loaded lap joint tends to produce high stresses at the ends of the joints due to the slight eccentricity of the force line. Excessive joint overlap also increases the stress concentrations at the joint ends.
- On lap joints the length of lap should be approximately 2.5 times that of the thinnest part for optimum strength. Increasing the width of the lap, adhesive thickness or increasing the stiffness of the parts to be joined can improve joint strength.
- Adhesive selection should be based on: joint type and loading, curing mechanism and operating conditions.
- Adhesives can be used to provide electrical, sound and heat insulation. Also, provides a barrier to prevent galvanic corrosion between dissimilar metals or to create a pressure tight seal.
- Design joints using minimum amount of adhesive and provide for uniform thin layers.
- Consideration of joint permanence is important for maintenance purposes.
- Jigs and fixtures should be used to maintain joint location during adhesive curing.
- Provision for the escape of gases and vapours in the design is important.
- Minimum sheet thickness = 0.05 mm.
- Maximum sheet thickness, commonly = 50 mm.
- Unequal thicknesses are common.

Quality issues

- Excellent quality joints with virtually no distortion can be produced.
- Stress distribution over the joint area is more uniform than other joining techniques.
- Joint fatigue resistance is improved due to inherent damping properties of adhesives.
- Heat sensitive materials can be joined without any change of base material properties.
- Dissimilar materials can cause residual stresses on cooling due to different expansion coefficients especially if heat is used in the curing process.
- Adhesives generally have a short shelf life.
- Optimum joint strength may not be immediate following assembly.
- Some adhesives can operate in temperatures up to approximately 250°C.
- Control of surface preparation, adhesive preparation, assembly environment and curing procedure is important for consistent joint quality.
- In surface preparation it is important to remove any contaminates from the joint area such as oxide layers, paint and thick films of grease and oil to aid 'wetting' of the joint. Mechanical abrasion, degreasing or chemical etching may be necessary depending on the base materials to be joined.
- Problems are encountered with materials with loose surface layers and materials prone to solvent attack, stress cracking, water migration or low surface energy.
- Joint inspection is difficult and quality control should include intermittent testing of joint strength.
- Joint strength may deteriorate with time and severe environmental conditions cause degradation.
- Rough surfaces are preferred to smooth ones to provide surface locking mechanisms.
- Fabrication tolerances are a function of the accuracy of the component parts and the assembly/jigging method.
- Joint surface free of irregular shapes and contours as produced by mechanical fastening techniques and welding.

6.10   Mechanical fastening

Process description

- Joining of parts by mechanical fastening systems which can be generally classified as being either permanent (no intention for later disassembly) or non-permanent (intention is for the later disassembly of parts for maintenance or inspection).

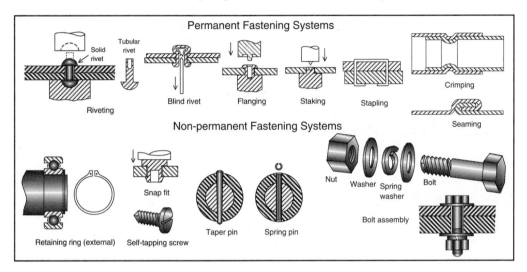

Materials

- Can join most materials and combinations of materials using various processes. Metals, plastics and ceramics are commonly joined.
- Fastening elements usually made from metal alloys (commonly medium carbon steel), but can also use plastics.
- Variety of coatings available for metal fasteners to improve corrosion resistance, commonly: zinc (electroplated and hot-dip), cadmium, chromate, phosphate and bluing.

Process variations

- Permanent fastening systems: rivets (solid, tubular, split and blind, explosive), staples, nails (wood and masonry), seaming, crimping, flanging, staking, interference and shrink fits.
- Non-permanent fastening systems: screws (wood, self-tapping, set, stud), expanding plugs for use with screws, threaded inserts, bolts and nuts (including a number of standard thread forms and a variety of drive types, locking mechanisms, washers and nuts), quick-acting mechanisms (cam lock), snap fits, locks, pins (dowel, taper, split, spring, cotter), retaining rings (internal and external, E-clip), keys (gib-head, taper), collets and sleeves (expanding, taper, Morse), expanding anchor bolts and rag bolts used for fastening to concrete.

- Can be manually or automatically performed, however, not all fastening processes lend themselves to automation easily.

Economic considerations

- High production rates are possible depending on the fastening system and degree of automation.
- Economical for very low production runs.
- All quantities.
- A smaller number of large fasteners may be more economical than many small ones.
- Tooling costs are low to high depending on degree of automation.
- Equipment costs are low.
- Direct labour costs are low to moderate. Cost of joint preparation can be high.
- Finishing costs are very low. Usually no finishing is required.

Typical applications

- Building structures.
- Automotive and aerospace assemblies and structures.
- Marine structures.
- Electronic assemblies and cabinets.
- Domestic appliances.
- Machinery.
- Furniture.

Design aspects

- All levels of complexity.
- Calculation of stresses in the fastener at the design stage is recommended in joints subjected to high static and/or dynamic loads.
- Examination of the stresses in the joint area under the fastener is important to determine the load bearing capability of the parts to be joined and the stress distributions.
- Recommended torque settings for bolted connections is critical for obtaining correct preloads.
- Provide for anti-vibration mechanisms in the fixing system (for example, lock nuts, spring washers) where necessary. Can also incorporate pressure tight seals and anti-corrosion materials.
- Try to use standard fastener sizes and lengths.
- Keep the number of fasteners to a minimum for economic reasons, however, for increased reliability when required, redundant fasteners should be considered.
- Design for the easy disassembly and maintenance of non-permanent fasteners, i.e. provide enough space for spanners, sockets and screwdrivers.
- Avoid placing fasteners too close to the edge of parts or too close to each other.
- When joining plastics it is good practice to use metal threaded inserts.
- Consideration of joint permanence is important for maintenance purposes.
- Minimum sheet thickness = 0.25 mm.

- Maximum section thickness, commonly = 200 mm.
- Unequal thicknesses are common.

Quality issues

- Galvanic corrosion between dissimilar metals requires careful consideration.
- There is a risk of damage to joined parts or fasteners when using permanent systems or non-permanent fasteners that have been disassembled many times.
- Stress relaxation can cause the joint to loosen over a period of time (especially in high temperature operating conditions) and subsequent re-torquing is recommended at regular intervals.
- Maximum operating temperatures of mechanical fastenings is approximately 700°C using nickel-chromium steel bolts.
- Machined thread forms are inherently weaker than rolled threads.
- Variations in flatness and squareness of abutment faces in assemblies can affect joint rigidity, corrosion resistance and sealing integrity.
- Lubricants and plate finishes on fasteners can help reduce torque required and further improve corrosion resistance.
- Stress concentrations in fastener and joint designs should be minimized by incorporating radii and gradual section changes.
- Hole design, preparation and size (if required) is important. Holes can act as stress concentrations. Can be overcome by inducing compressive residual stresses in the hole to improve fatigue life.
- Fabrication tolerances are a function of the accuracy of the component parts and the fastening system used.

2.4 Combining the use of the matrix and PRIMAs

Consider the problem of a designer wanting to know which manufacturing process to specify for the manufacture of a tub shaped product of 2 mm uniform thickness, 1 m length and 0.5 m in depth and width made from a thermoplastic with an annual production quantity of approximately 5000. The PRIMA selection matrix in Figure 2.1 shows that there are four processes [2.1] to [2.4] considered economically viable given this level of detail, these are: injection moulding, compression moulding, vacuum forming and blow moulding respectively. The designer would then proceed to the manufacturing process PRIMAs for the above processes. Comparing data, vacuum forming would be chosen as it is suited to the manufacture of tub shaped parts of uniform thickness within this size range, also being relatively inexpensive with a high production rate.

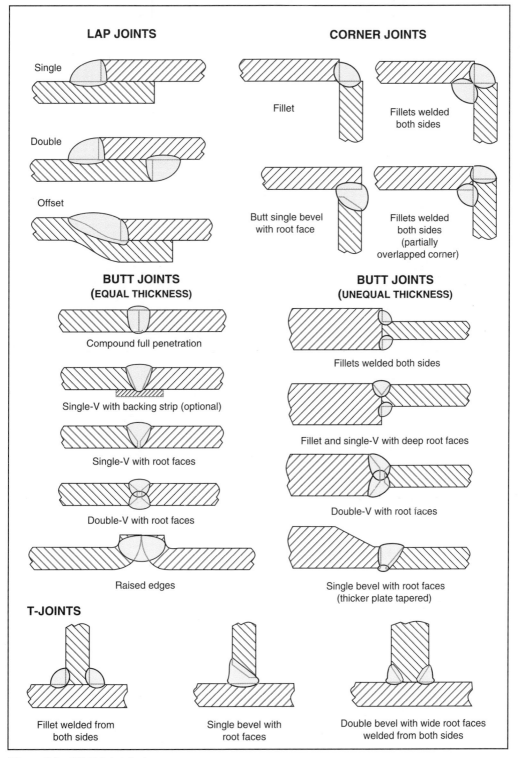

Figure 2.2 Weld joint design

Part III
Costing designs

A procedure to enable the exploration of design and process combinations for manufacturing cost.

3.1 Introduction

For financial control and successful marketing it is necessary to have cost targets and realizations throughout the product introduction process. Product cost is virtually always a prime element in decision making in manufacturing industry. The main problem in product introduction is the provision of reliable cost information in the early stages of the design process for the comparison of alternative conceptual designs and assessment of the myriad of ways in which a product may be structured during concept development.

Cost estimates are needed to determine the viability of projects and to minimize project and product costs. The inadequate nature of the historical standard costing methods and cost estimating practices found in most companies has been highlighted by researchers over a number of years (3.1–3.3).

One signal that emerges from all workers is that it is crucial to reject uneconomic designs early, for it is not often possible to reduce costs productively once production has commenced largely due to the high cost of change at this stage in the product life cycle. Hence cost analysis is best utilized at the stage in the design process when rough designs for a component have been prepared.

The aim of the costing analysis presented here (3.4–3.5) is to highlight expensive and difficult to manufacture designs, thus indicating areas that will benefit from further attention before the design has been completed.

Benefits of the methodology include:

- Lower component costs.
- Systematic component costing.
- Identification of feasible manufacturing processes.
- Rapid comparison of alternative designs and competitor products.
- Reduced engineering change.
- Shorter development time and reduced time to market.
- Education and training.

The methodology described is ideally applicable to team-based applications, both manually and in the form of computer software. The work was primarily designed to cater for components found in the light engineering, aerospace and automotive business sectors.

3.2 Design costing methodology

In order to produce a practical and widely applicable tool for designers with the capability to provide feedback on the technological and economic consequences of component design decisions, it was considered useful to develop a sample model that is widely applicable to a number of different manufacturing processes. In addition, the model was designed such that appropriate manufacturing processes and equipment requirements can be specified early in the product introduction process.

Recognizing the problem that the relationship between a design and its manufacturing feasibility and cost is not easily amenable to precise scientific formulation, the model has come out of knowledge engineering work in a number of user companies and those specializing in particular manufacturing techniques.

3.2.1 Development of the model

The model is logically based on material volume and processing considerations. The process cost is determined using a basic processing cost (the cost of producing an ideal design for that process) and design-dependent relative cost coefficients (which enable any component design to be compared with the ideal). Material costs are calculated taking into account the transformation of material to yield the final form.

Thus a single process model for manufacturing cost (Mi) can be formulated as:

$$Mi = V\,Cmt + Rc\,Pc \tag{1}$$

where

V = volume of material required in order to produce the component
Cmt = cost of the material per unit volume in the required form
Pc = basic processing cost for an ideal design of component by a specific process
Rc = relative cost coefficient assigned to a component design (taking account of shape complexity, suitability of material for processing, section dimensions, tolerances and surface finish).

The initial hypothesis can be expanded to allow for secondary processing and thus the model can take the general form:

$$Mi = V\,Cmt + (Rc_1\,Pc_1 + Rc_2\,Pc_2 + ... + Rc_n Pc_n)$$

$$Mi = V\,Cmt + \sum_{i=1}^{n} Rc_{(i)}\,Pc_{(i)} \tag{2}$$

where

n = number of operations required to achieve the finished component

In order for such a formulation to be used in practice it is necessary to define relationships enabling the determination of the quantities Pc and Rc for design-process combinations. In practice it has been found that equation [1] is the form preferred by industry. This is based on the need to work in the early stages of the design process with incomplete component data and without the necessity for detailing the sequence of manufacturing operations. The approach has been to build the secondary processing requirements into the relative cost coefficient. More will be said about this in Section 3.2.3.

3.2.2 Basic processing cost (Pc)

In order to represent the basic processing cost of an ideal design for a particular process, it is first necessary to identify the factors on which it is dependent. These factors include:

- Equipment costs including installation.
- Operating costs: labour, number of shifts worked, supervision and overheads, etc.
- Processing times.
- Tooling costs.
- Component demand.

The above variables are taken account of in the calculation of *Pc* using the simple equation:

$$Pc = \alpha T + \beta/N \qquad [3]$$

where

α = cost of setting up and operating a specific process, including plant, labour, supervision and overheads, per second

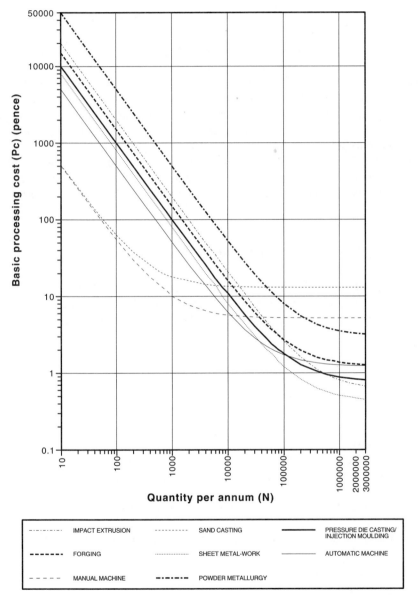

Figure 3.1   Basic processing cost (*Pc*) against annual production quantity (*N*) for some selected manufacturing processes

β = process specific total tooling cost for an ideal design
T = process time in seconds for processing an ideal design of component by a specific
   process
N = total component demand.

Values for α and β are based on expertise from companies specializing in producing components in specific technological areas. Using these process specific values in equation [3], it is possible to produce comparative cost curves for any process.

A sample set of data for Pc against annual production quantity for nine common manufacturing processes, based on one working shift per day and two-year depreciation/payback, is illustrated in Figure 3.1. While the above average values might be adequate in some cases, the methodology was devised with the idea that users would develop their own data for the process they would wish to consider. Such an approach has many benefits to a business, including ownership of the data and a confidence in the results produced. The values of Pc represent the minimum likely costs associated with a particular manufacturing process at a given annual production quantity. In this way the process selection map in Figure 3.1 can indicate the lowest likely cost for a component associated with a particular manufacturing process route assuming an ideal design for the process, one shift working and a two-year payback on investment.

Having defined Pc it is necessary to determine the design-dependent factors. The variables; shape complexity, tolerances, etc., modify the relationship between the curves. The relative cost coefficient Rc in equation (1) is one way in which these variables can be expressed.

3.2.3   Relative cost coefficient (Rc)

This coefficient will determine how much more expensive it will be to produce a component with more demanding features than the 'ideal design'. The characteristics which we have assumed to influence the relative cost coefficient, Rc, are given below:

$$Rc = \phi(Cmp, Cc, Cs, Ct, Cf)$$

where

   Cmp = relative cost associated with material-process suitability
   Cc = relative cost associated with producing components of different geometrical
      complexity
   Cs = relative cost associated with size considerations and achieving component section reductions/thickness
   Ct = relative cost associated with obtaining a specified tolerance
   Cf = relative cost associated with obtaining a specified surface finish.

Analysis of the influence of the above quantities and discussions with experts led to the idea that these could be combined as shown below:

$$Rc = Cmp^a \ Cc^b \ Cs^c \ Ct^d \ Cf^e \qquad (4)$$

where a, b, c, d and e are weighting exponents.

However, it was found that the knowledge could be structured to enable each of the exponents to be assigned the value of unity. Therefore, the relative cost coefficient can be represented by the formula:

$$Rc \quad = \quad Cmp \; Cc \; Cs \; Cft \tag{5}$$

where *Cft* is the higher of *Cf* and *Ct*, but not both. This was refined on the basis that when a fine surface finish is being produced, fine tolerances could be attained at the same time and thus it would be somewhat dubious to compound both relative cost coefficients.

Knowledge engineering indicated that equation (5) was the most appropriate combination of coefficients at the present stage of development. The method of comparison and accumulation of costs was shown to be analogous to those methodologies employed by experts in the field of cost engineering/estimating. For the ideal design each of these coefficients is unity, but as the component design moves away from this state then one or more of the coefficients may increase in magnitude, thus changing the manufacturing cost term, *Mi*, in equation (1).

Figure 3.2 shows how the cost curves for *Pc* (see Figure 3.1) are modified according to the model proposed as a component design shifts away from the ideal for that process. As the design becomes more difficult to process, because material or geometrical changes for example, its cost curve progresses up the cost axis along the lines illustrated in the figure.

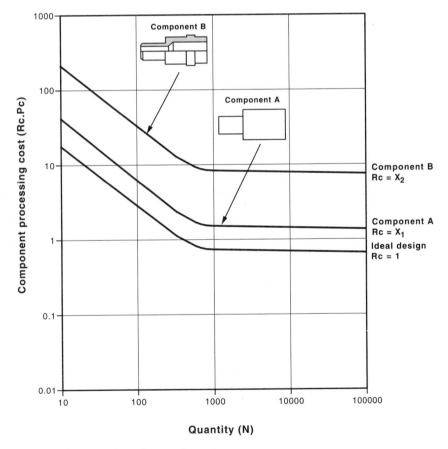

Figure 3.2   Relative manufacturing cost/quantity curves

Sets of data for the above relative cost coefficients Cmp, Cc, Cs, Ct and Cf can be found in Figures 3.3, 3.4, 3.5 and 3.6 respectively.

Material to process suitability (Cmp)
In Figure 3.3 the *Cmp* data indicates the suitability of using various materials with different processes. Clearly some combinations are inappropriate and *Cmp* values only appear at nodes currently considered to be technologically and economically feasible.

Shape complexity (Cc)
Figure 3.4(a) presents a system of shape classification for the determination of *Cc*. The first step is to determine the basic shape category. There are three basic shape categories: solid of revolution, prismatic solid and flat or thin-wall section components. The above classes are divided into five bands of complexity.

The classification process must reflect the finished form of the component and the features listed in the tables should be used as an aid to the selection of the appropriate value of *Cc*. Shape complexity definitions are also included the Figure 3.4(b).

Determination of shape complexity is important. Failure to classify the geometry properly may affect the end result (*Mi*) quite significantly, and studying the shape complexity definitions is crucial in this connection.

Section thickness (Cs)
Figure 3.5 shows the relative cost consequences of producing specific section/wall thickness for our sample set of processes. If the required section falls to the left of the shaded line an additional machining/grinding process is likely to be necessary and this is included in the indices given.

PROCESS / MATERIAL	IMPACT EXTRUSION	SAND CASTING	PRESSURE DIE CASTING	FORGING	SHEET METAL-WORK	MACHINING	POWDER METALLURGY	INJECTION MOULDING
CAST IRON		1				1.2	1.6	
LOW CARBON STEEL	1.3	1.2		1	1.2	1.4	1.2	
ALLOY STEEL	2	1.3		2	1.5	2.5	1.1	
STAINLESS STEEL	2	1.5		2	1.5	4	1.1	
COPPER ALLOY	1	1	3	1	1	1.1	1	
ALUMINIUM ALLOY	1	1	1.5	1	1	1	1	
ZINC ALLOY	1	1	1.2	1	1	1.1	1	
THERMOPLASTIC						1.1		1
THERMOSET						1.2		1
ELASTOMERS						1.1		1.5

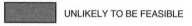 UNLIKELY TO BE FEASIBLE

Figure 3.3 Relative cost data for material processing suitability (*Cmp*)

Notes - Geometrical Considerations

The shape complexity index is obtained by using a feature based classification system which enables the important design/manufacturing issues to be taken into account. Firstly determine the shape category:

A	B	C
Part envelope is largely a solid of revolution	Part envelope is largely a prismatic solid	Flat or thin wall section component

Within the above classes, components are divided into five bands of complexity.

Note that the classification process should reflect the finished form of the component and the features listed in the tables should be used to aid the selection of the appropriate band. Always determine the classification by working from the left hand side of the table.

Notes - Shape Complexity Definitions

- **Basic Features** - Straight forward processing where the operation can be carried out without a change of setting or the need of complex tooling. Parts are usually uniform in cross section.

- **Secondary Features** - As above, but where additional processing is necessary or more complex tooling is required.

- **Multi-axis Features** - Parts require to be processed in more than a single axis/set-up.

- **Non-uniform Features** - Parts require the development of more complex processing techniques/set-up.

- **Complex Forms** - Parts need dedicated tooling and the development of specialised processing techniques.

- **Single Axis** - This is usually the axis along the components largest dimension, however, in the case of cylindrical or disc shaped components, it is more convenient to consider the axis of revolution as the primary axis.

- **Through Features** - Features which run along, across or through a component from one end or side to the other.

- **Important** - If the component falls into more than one category, always choose the one that gives the highest value of Cc.

Figure 3.4a Notes on shape classifications used in the determination of *Cc*

A — Part Envelope is Largely a Solid of Revolution

Single/Primary Axis		Secondary Axes: Straight line features parallel and/or perpendicular to primary axis		Complex Forms
Basic rotational features only	Regular secondary/ repetitive features	Interna	Internal and/or external features	Irregular and/or complex forms.
A 1	A 2	A 3	A 4	A 5
Category Includes: Rotationally symmetrical/ grooves, undercuts, steps, chamfers, tapers and holes along the primary axis/centre line	Internal/external threads, knurling and simple contours through flats/splines/keyways on/around the primary axis/centre line	Holes/threads/ counterbores and other internal features not on the primary axis	Projections, complex features, blind flats, splines, keyways on secondary axes	Complex contoured surfaces,and /or series of features which are not represented in previous categories

B — Part Envelope is Largely a Rectangular or Cubic Prism

Single Axis/Plane		Multiple Axes		Complex Forms
Basic features only	Regular secondary/ repetitive features	Orthogonal/straight line based features	Simple curved features on a single plane	Irregular and/or contoured forms
B 1	B 2	B 3	B 4	B 5
Category Includes: Through steps, chamfers and grooves/channels/slots and holes/threads on a single axis	Regular through features, T-slots and racks/plain gear sections etc. Repetitive holes/threads/counter bores on a single plane	Regular orthogonal/straight line based pockets and/or projections on one or more axis. Angled holes/threads/ counter bores	Curves on internal and/or external surfaces	Complex 3-D contoured surfaces/geometries which cannot be assigned to previous categories.

C — Flat Or Thin Wall Section Components

Single Axis	Secondary/Repetitive Regular Features		Regular Forms	Complex Forms
Basic features only	Uniform section/ wall thickness	Non-uniform section/ wall thickness	Cup, cone and box-type parts	Non-uniform and/or contoured forms
C 1	C 2	C 3	C 4	C 5
Category Includes: Blanks, washers, simple bends, forms and through features on or parallel to primary axis	Plain cogs/gears, multiple or continuous bends and forms	Component section changes not made up of multiple bends or forms. Steps, tapers and blind features	Components may involve changes in section thickness	Complex or irregular features or series of features which are not represented in previous categories

Figure 3.4b Shape classifications used in the determination of *Cc*

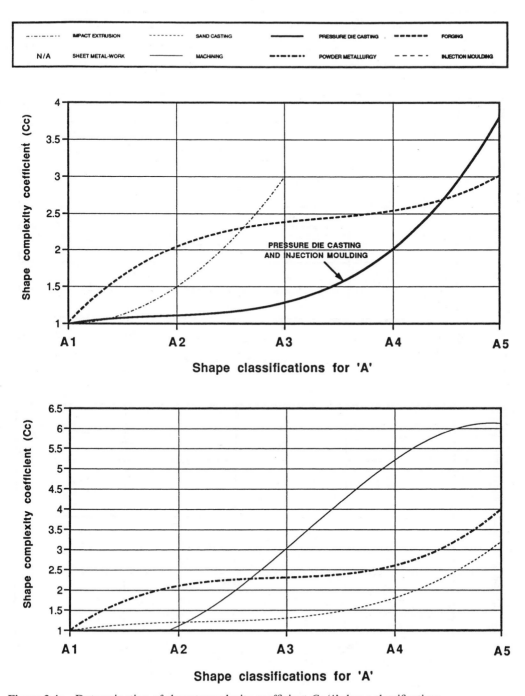

Figure 3.4c   Determination of shape complexity coefficient *Cc* 'A' shape classifications

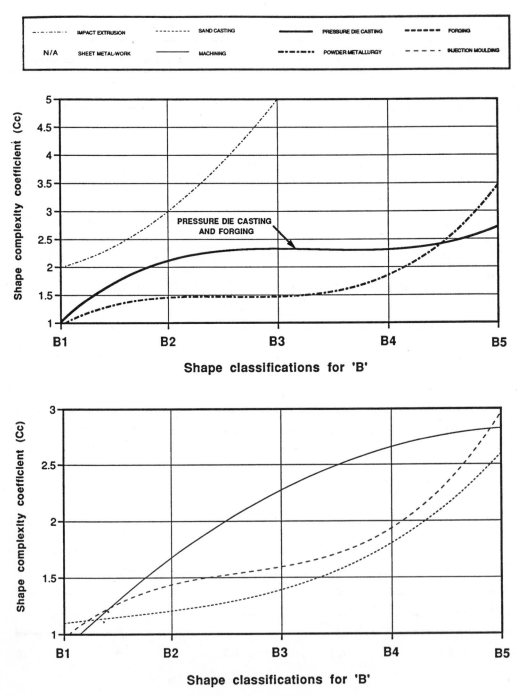

Figure 3.4d Determination of shape complexity coefficient *Cc* for 'B' shape classifications

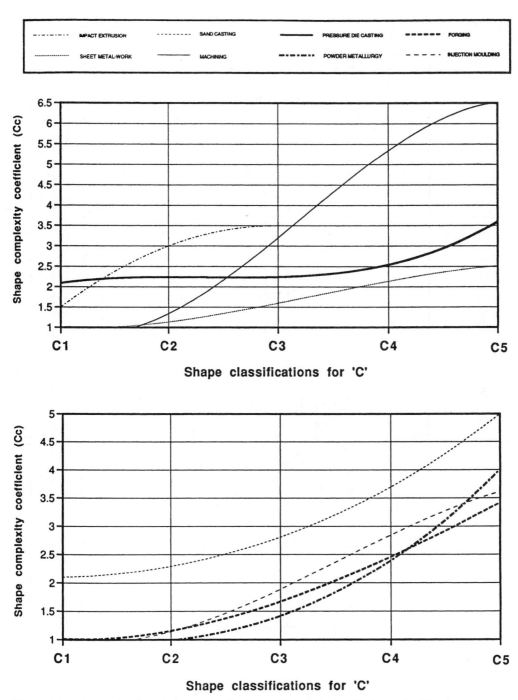

Figure 3.4e Determination of shape complexity coefficient *Cc* for 'C' shape classifications

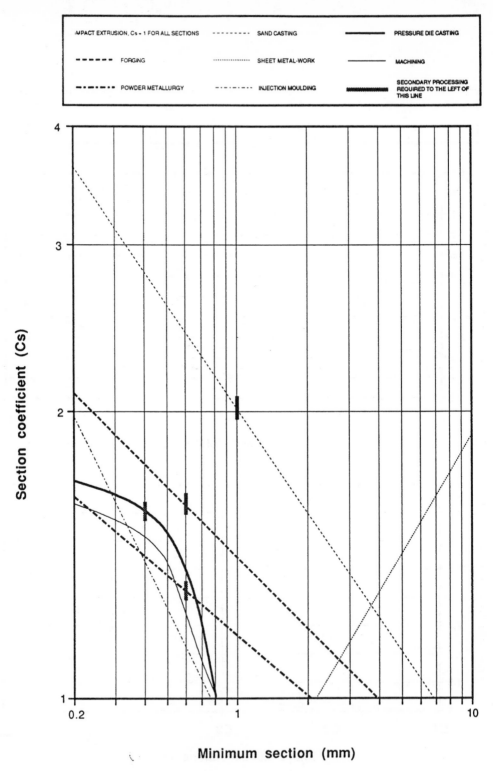

Figure 3.5 Chart used for the determination of the section coefficient *Cs*

(Overall size considerations for components are not included in the sample data. Using a process outside its normal size domain can result in an additional cost (3.6). In the situation where a process is being considered for a component that is longer or smaller than the size range given in the macro (length, area, volume or weight) the estimate of cost produced is likely to be a lower bound value.)

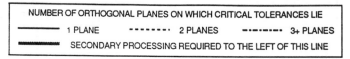

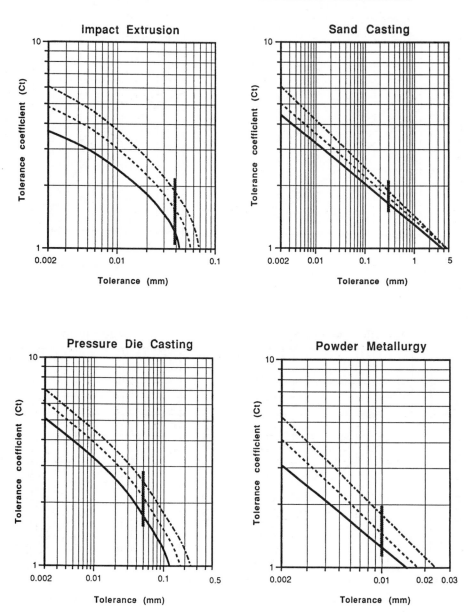

Figure 3.6a Graphs for the determination of the tolerance coefficient *Ct*

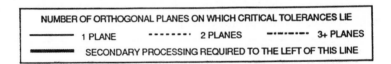

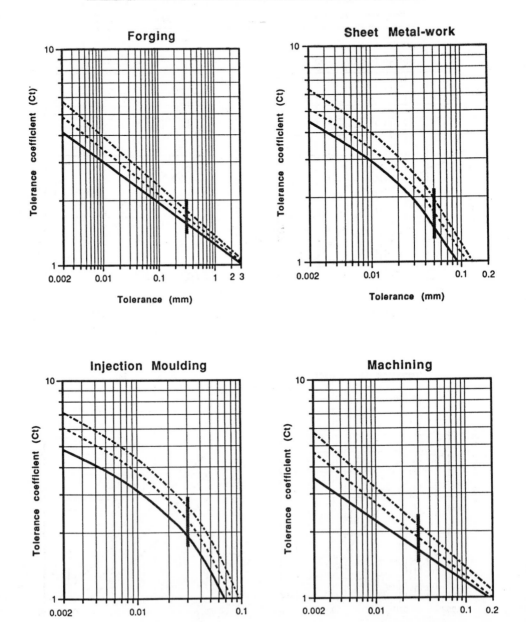

Figure 3.6b Graphs for the determination of the tolerance coefficient C_t

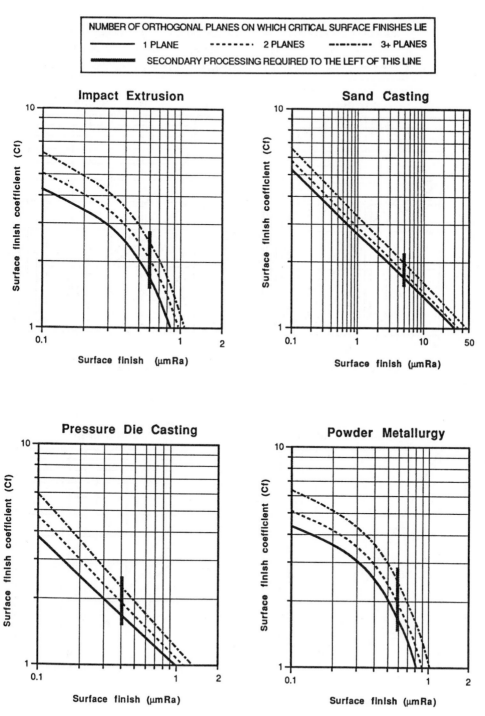

Figure 3.6c   Graphs for the determination of the surface finish coefficient *Cs*

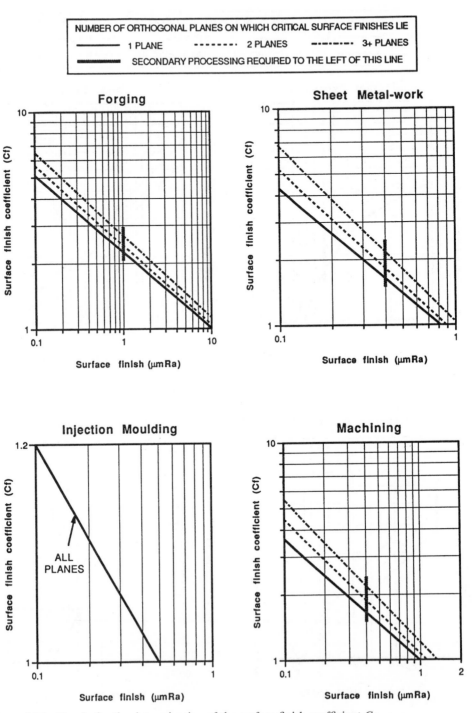

Figure 3.6d Graphs for the determination of the surface finish coefficient *Cs*

Tolerance (Ct) and surface finish (Cf)

The sample data on the affects of tolerance *(Ct)* and surface finish *(Cf)* can be found in Figures 3.6(a) and (b) and 3.6(c) and (d) respectively. The figure indicates the relative cost consequences of achieving specific tolerance and surface finish levels for the various manufacturing processes.

The process of analysis is:

1. determine the most important tolerance values
2. identify the tolerance band on the *Ct* table
3. count the number of tolerances in the same band
4. identify the number of planes on which the critical values lie
5. select the appropriate *Ct* index from the table.

If the tolerance falls to the left of the shaded line, a final machining, lapping, honing, polishing or grinding process is necessary to achieve the tolerance. This is already taken into account of in the indices shown. Only the tightest tolerance required should be used, even if it only occurs one one plane.

Included in the graph are separate lines for the number of orthogonal axes or planes (either 1, 2 or 3+) on which the critical tolerances lie, and which cannot be achieved from a single direction using the manufacturing process.

Repeat the above process exactly for *Cf* using the graphs in Figures 3.6(c) and (d). Note that *Cft* = *Ct* **or** *Cf*, which ever gives the highest value.

3.2.4 Material cost *(Mc)*

The material cost *(Mc)* was defined in equation (1) as the volume of raw material required to process the component multiplied by the cost of the material per unit volume in the required form *(Cmt)*:

MATERIAL		Cmt^*
CAST IRON		0.00045
LOW CARBON STEEL		0.00039
ALLOY STEEL		0.00148
STAINLESS STEEL		0.00195
COPPER ALLOY		0.00245
ALUMINIUM ALLOY		0.00078
ZINC ALLOY		0.00117
THERMOPLASTIC	- NYLON, PMMA	0.00061
	OTHER	0.00017
THERMOSET		0.00033
ELASTOMERS		0.00017

* Cmt is based on cost per unit volume (pence/mm³)

Figure 3.7 Sample material cost values per unit volume *(Cmt)* for commonly used material classes

$$Mc = V\, Cmt \qquad\qquad (6)$$

Sample average values for Cmt for commonly used material classes can be found in Figure 3.7. Company specific data should be used wherever possible.

Component manufacture may involve surface coating and/or heat treatments, and have some effect on manufacturing cost. Development of models for this aspect of component manufacturing cost are in progress (3.7).

In material selection, recycling of materials is increasing in importance and should be given due consideration. For more information on material selection the reader is referred to references (3.8–3.10).

Note that the volume (V) in equation (1) must be worked out in cubic millimetres (mm^3).

In many situations the material cost can form a large proportion of the total component cost, therefore a consistent approach should be taken in the volume calculation if valid comparisons are to be produced.

The volume may be calculated in one of two ways:

1. Using the input (total) volume – If the total volume of material required to produce the component is known (i.e. the volume including any processing waste) then this value is used for V and the waste coefficient is ignored.
2. Using the final (finished) volume – If the amount of waste material is not known, then the final component volume may be used. In this case, use a waste coefficient (Wc) which takes into account the waste material consumed by a particular process. The formulation for V for this method is:

$$V = Vf\, Wc \qquad\qquad (7)$$

where

PROCESS	WASTE COEFFICIENT (Wc)
IMPACT EXTRUSION	1.0
FORGING	1.2
SHEET METAL-WORK	1.2
SAND CASTING	1.25
PRESSURE DIE CASTING	1.15
POWDER METALLURGY	1.05
INJECTION MOULDING	1.1
MANUAL AND AUTOMATIC MACHINING	**NOT APPLICABLE** Calculate initial volume (V)

Figure 3.8 Approximate values for waste coefficient

Vf = finished volume of the component.

Some typical waste coefficients for the sample of processes can be found in Figure 3.8. While in many cases the values quoted can be used with confidence, estimation of the input volume to the process is the approach preferred (method 1).

In many applications, when calculating the volume of a component, it is not always necessary to go into great detail. Approximate methods are often satisfactory when comparing designs and it can be helpful if a design is broken down into simple shape elements allowing the quick calculation of a volume.

Before looking at the industrial applications of the design costing methodology it should be noted that material and process selection need to be considered together, they should not be viewed in isolation. The analysis presented here does not in any way take into account physical properties such as strength, weight, conductivity, etc.

3.3   Industrial applications

3.3.1   Model validation

In order to validate the approach, a number of companies were consulted covering a wide range of manufacturing technology and products. Understandably, often companies were reluctant to discuss cost information, even admitting that they had no systematic process or structure to the way new jobs were priced, relying almost exclusively on the knowledge and expertise of one or two senior estimators. However, a number of companies were able to provide both estimated and actual cost data for a sufficient range of components to perform some meaningful validation.

Figure 3.9(a) illustrates the results of a validation exercise in a company producing plastic moulded components. The analysis was performed on a number of products at random and the estimated costs predicted by the evaluation, *Mi*, have been plotted against the actual manufacturing costs provided by the company. Figure 3.9(b) illustrates another plot, this time from a company producing pressed sheet metal parts. Figure 3.10 illustrates some of the components included in the validation studies.

Validation exercises on a range of component types which was carried out by 22 individuals in industry (mechanical, electrical and manufacturing engineers) showed that the main variability encountered was in the calculation of component volume and in the assignment of the shape complexity index (3.11). While the determination of component volume is mechanistic, it is recognized that the determination of the most appropriate shape complexity classification requires judgmental skills and experience in the application of the methodology. These problems were largely eliminated when the analysis was carried out in a team environment, where highly consistent and reliable results were produced.

In addition, training in the application of the methodology yields considerable improvements in the quality and consistency of the results produced. Giving training and operation in a team situation the methodology has proved capable of predicting the cost of manufacture for a component to better than 16%.

Customizing the data to particular businesses would significantly enhance the accuracy of the predicted costs obtained from the analysis.

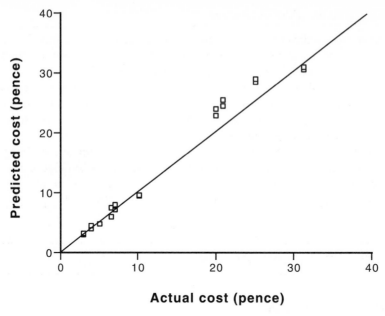

Figure 3.9a Cost validation results for injection moulded components

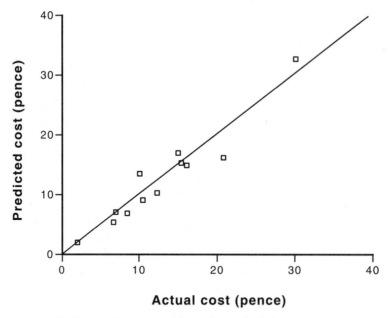

Figure 3.9b Cost validation results for pressed steel components

3.3.2 Modes of application

Under this heading we will say more about applications of the cost analysis and illustrate this through a number of examples. One of the primary goals of the technique was to

Figure 3.10 Examples of components included in the validation studies

enable a product team to anticipate the cost of manufacture associated with alternative component design solutions, resulting from the activities of design for assembly (DFA). (The technique is currently used to augment the DFA method exploited commercially by CSC Manufacturing in the form of DFA consulting projects and as part of the simultaneous engineering tools and techniques software 'TeamSET' (3.12, 3.13).)

As mentioned earlier, one of the main objectives of DFA is the reduction of component numbers in a product to minimize assembly cost. This tends to generate product design solutions that contain fewer but sometimes more complex components embodying a number of functions. Such an approach is often criticized as being sub-optimal; therefore it is important to know the consequences of such moves on component manufacturing costs.

An illustration of how the design costing analysis can be used in DFA is given in Figures 3.11 and 3.12. Figure 3.11(a) shows the original design of a trim screw assembly and Figure 3.11(b) the replacement design. The DFA analyses can be seen in Figure 3.12 (a) and (b), respectively. Notice that these figures include data on manufacturing cost. A breakdown of the cost analysis for the two components in the new design of the trim screw is given in Figure 3.13.

Each component has been assigned a manufacturing index which is representative of a cost in pence. Figure 3.12(c) provides a summary of the resulting measures of performance for each design. Again manufacturing cost values have been included. It can be seen from this that it is possible to fully assess the production cost consequences of each design in terms of both component manufacturer and assembly. Note that the total component manufacturing costs associated with the new design resulting from DFA are less than in the original: this turns out to be the case in many of the DFA studies examined to date by the authors.

A simple illustration of a case where the situation is not quite so clear cut is given in Figure 3.14. The DFA approach drives consideration of the assembly design proposal shown in design 'B'. An investigation of the two designs using the cost analysis suggests that from a component manufacturing point of view design 'A' represents a cost saving.

In this example the same manufacturing process (machining) is used for both pin

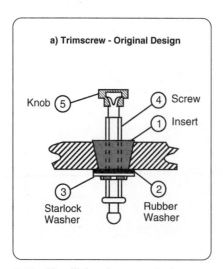
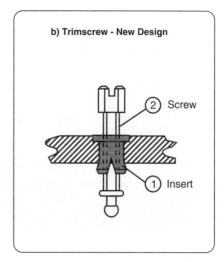

Figure 3.11   Headlight trim screw designs

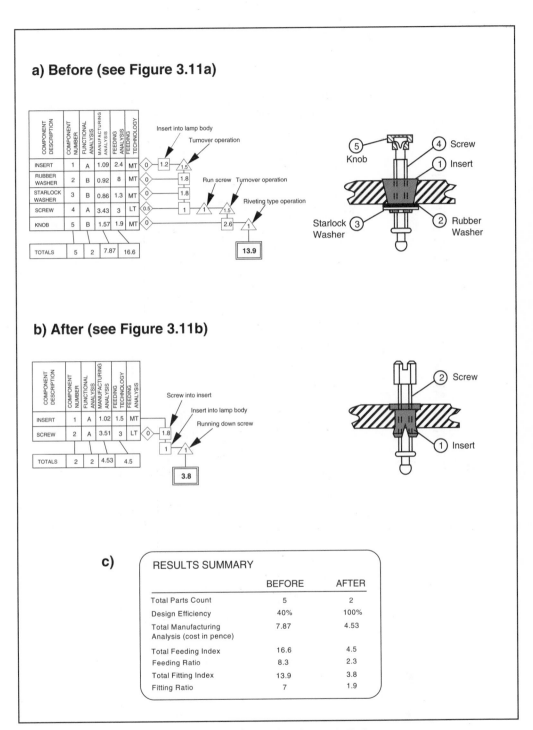

a) Before (see Figure 3.11a)

COMPONENT DESCRIPTION	COMPONENT NUMBER	FUNCTIONAL ANALYSIS	MANUFACTURING ANALYSIS	FEEDING ANALYSIS	FEEDING TECHNOLOGY
INSERT	1	A	1.09	2.4	MT
RUBBER WASHER	2	B	0.92	8	MT
STARLOCK WASHER	3	B	0.86	1.3	MT
SCREW	4	A	3.43	3	LT
KNOB	5	B	1.57	1.9	MT
TOTALS	5	2	7.87	16.6	

Insert into lamp body
Turnover operation
Run screw   Turnover operation
Riveting type operation

1.2   1.5
1.8
1.8
0.5   1   1   1.5
2.6   1

13.9

5 Knob   4 Screw
1 Insert
Starlock 3 Washer
2 Rubber Washer

b) After (see Figure 3.11b)

COMPONENT DESCRIPTION	COMPONENT NUMBER	FUNCTIONAL ANALYSIS	MANUFACTURING ANALYSIS	FEEDING TECHNOLOGY	FEEDING ANALYSIS
INSERT	1	A	1.02	1.5	MT
SCREW	2	A	3.51	3	LT
TOTALS	2	2	4.53	4.5	

Screw into insert
Insert into lamp body
Running down screw

1.8
1   1

3.8

2 Screw
1 Insert

c)

RESULTS SUMMARY

	BEFORE	AFTER
Total Parts Count	5	2
Design Efficiency	40%	100%
Total Manufacturing Analysis (cost in pence)	7.87	4.53
Total Feeding Index	16.6	4.5
Feeding Ratio	8.3	2.3
Total Fitting Index	13.9	3.8
Fitting Ratio	7	1.9

Figure 3.12   Before and after analysis of a headlight trim screw design

MANUFACTURING ANALYSIS (Mi RESULTS) TABLE

PRODUCT NAME: TRIMSCREW

PRODUCT CODE / ID: NEW DESIGN

PRODUCT QUANTITY: 1,000,000 pa

COMPONENT DETAILS					Mc = V x Cmt x [Wc]				(A)		Rc = Cc x Cmp x Cs x [Ctf]										(B)	(A) + (B)
PART No.	PART ID	PART DESCRIPTION	MATERIAL	PRIMARY PROCESS	SHAPE COMP.	Volume (mm^3)	Cmt	Wc*	Mc	Pc	Cc	Cmp	Section (mm)	Cs	Toler-ance (mm)	Ct	Surface Finish (µmRa)	Cf	Ctf	Rc	(Pc x Rc)	Mi (cost in pence)
1		INSERT	THERMOPLASTIC	INJ. MOULDING	A1	626	0.00017	1.1	0.117	0.9	1	1	1	1	0.1	1	3.2	1	1	1	0.9	1.02
2		SCREW	LOW CARB. STEEL	MACHINING	A2	4262	0.00039	-	1.66	1.2	1.1	1.4	2	1	0.1	1	3.2	1	1	1.54	1.85	3.51
					SHAPE CLASSIFICATION (FIGURE 3.4 a)		MATERIAL COST (FIGURE 3.7)	WASTE COEFFICIENT (FIGURE 3.8)		BASIC PROCESSING COST (FIGURE 3.1)	SHAPE COMPLEXITY COEFFICIENT (FIGURE 3.8)	MATERIAL TO PROCESS SUITABILITY COEFFICIENT (FIGURE 3.3)		MINIMUM SECTION COEFFICIENT (FIGURE 3.5)		TOLERANCE COEFFICIENT (FIGURE 3.6 a & b)		SURFACE FINISH COEFFICIENT (FIGURE 3.6 c & d)			TOTAL	4.53

* Not applicable to machining

Figure 3.13 Cost analysis for the manufacture of components in the new trim screw design

MANUFACTURING ANALYSIS (Mi RESULTS) TABLE

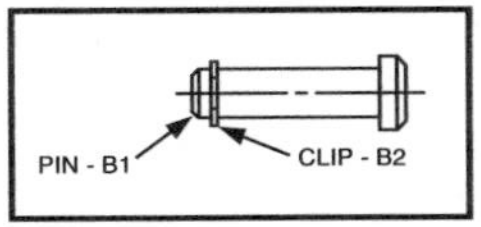

PRODUCT NAME: PIVOT PIN
PRODUCT CODE / ID: DESIGNS A AND B
PRODUCT QUANTITY: 30,000 pa

DESIGN A

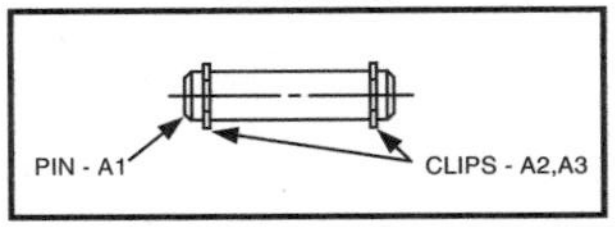

PIN - A1
CLIPS - A2,A3

DESIGN B

PIN - B1
CLIP - B2

	COMPONENT DETAILS				Mc = V x Cmt x [Wc]			(A) Mc	Pc	Rc = Cc x Cmp x Cs x [Ctf]									Rc	(B) (Pc x Rc)	(A)+(B) Mi (cost in pence)
PART No. ID	PART DESCRIPTION	MATERIAL	PRIMARY PROCESS	SHAPE COMP.	Volume (mm³)	Cmt	Wc*			Cc	Cmp	Section (mm)	Cs	Tolerance (mm)	Ct	Surface Finish (μmRa)	Cf	Ctf			
DESIGN A																					
A1	PIN	ALLOY STEEL	MACHINING	A1	4850	0.00148	-	7.2	3	1	1.5	5	1	0.1	1.1	3.2	1	1	1.65	4.95	12.15
A2	CLIP	STAINLESS STEEL	SHEET METAL-WORK																		1.4**
A3	CLIP	STAINLESS STEEL	SHEET METAL-WORK																		1.4**
																				TOTAL	14.95
DESIGN B																					
B1	PIN	ALLOY STEEL	MACHINING	A1	9900	0.00148	-	14.7	3	1	1.5	5	1	0.1	1.1	3.2	1	1	1.65	4.95	19.65
B2	CLIP	STAINLESS STEEL	SHEET METAL-WORK																		1.8**
																				TOTAL	21.45

* Not applicable to machining
** Supplier quotation

Figure 3.14 Estimated costs for alternative designs of pivot pin components

designs and the difference in cost results from the different material volume requirements. (The values of *Pc* (3) and *Rc* (1.65) are the same in each case.) Supplier cost data is used in the case of the standard clip fasteners. Hence, selection on the basis of cost demands a trade-off between assembly and manufacturing cost. Both design solutions are commonly seen in products from various business sectors and product groups.

MANUFACTURING ANALYSIS (Mi RESULTS) TABLE

PLUG BODY

PRODUCT NAME: PLUG BODY
PRODUCT CODE / ID: _____
PRODUCT QUANTITY: 1,000,000 pa

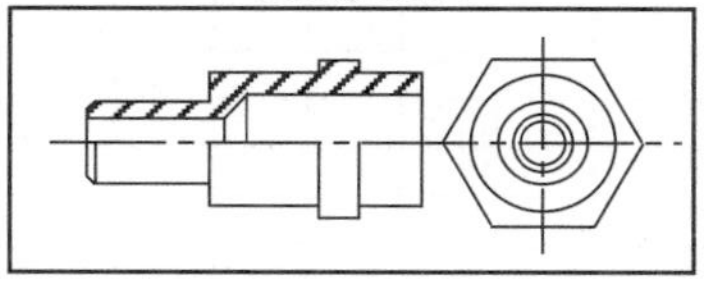

COMPONENT DETAILS

| | | | | | Mc = V x Cmt x [Wc] | | | (A) | | Rc = Cc x Cmp x Cs x [Ctf] | | | | | | | | | | (B) | (A)+(B) |
PART No. ID	PART DESCRIPTION	MATERIAL	PRIMARY PROCESS	SHAPE COMP.	Volume (mm³)	Cmt	Wc*	Mc	Pc	Cc	Cmp	Section (mm)	Cs	Tolerance (mm)	Ct	Surface Finish (μmRa)	Cf	Ctf	Rc	(Pc x Rc)	Mi (cost in pence)
AT 1,000,000 pa																					
1	PLUG BODY	LOW CARB. STEEL	MACHINING	A2	22100	0.00039	-	8.62	1.2	1.1	1.4	1.5	1	0.2	1	3.2	1	1	1.54	1.85	10.47
1	PLUG BODY	LOW CARB. STEEL	IMPACT EXTRUSION	A2	3860	0.00039	1	1.51	0.8	1	1.3	1.5	1	0.2	1	3.2	1	1	1.3	1.04	2.55
AT 20,000 pa																					
1	PLUG BODY	LOW CARB. STEEL	MACHINING	A2	22100	0.00039	-	8.62	3.5	1.1	1.4	1.5	1	0.2	1	3.2	1	1	1.54	5.39	14.01
1	PLUG BODY	LOW CARB. STEEL	IMPACT EXTRUSION	A2	3860	0.00039	1	1.51	11	1	1.3	1.5	1	0.2	1	3.2	1	1	1.3	14.3	15.8

* Not applicable to machining

Figure 3.15 Comparison of automatic machining and impact extrusion processes for the manufacture of a plug body

MANUFACTURING ANALYSIS (Mi RESULTS) TABLE

PRODUCT NAME   CONTROL VALVE SLEEVE

PRODUCT CODE / ID   -

PRODUCT QUANTITY   80,000 pa

CONTROL VALVE SLEEVE

Surface finish in bore = 0.4μmRa

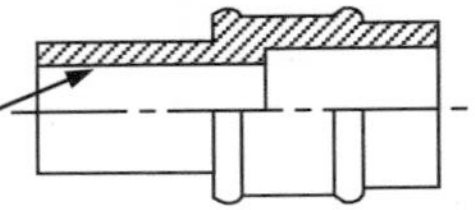

COMPONENT DETAILS				$Mc = V \times Cmt \times [Wc]$						$Rc = Cc \times Cmp \times Cs \times [Ctf]$										(A)+(B)
								(A)										**(B)**		**Mi**
PART No.	ID	PART DESCRIPTION	MATERIAL	PRIMARY PROCESS	SHAPE COMP.	Volume (mm³)	Cmt	Wc	**Mc**	**Pc**	Cc	Cmp	Section (mm)	Cs	Toler-ance (mm)	Ct	Surface Finish (μmRa)	Cf	Ctf	**Rc**	(Pc x Rc)	(cost in pence)
1		SLEEVE	ALUMINIUM	PRES. DIE CASTING	A1	5600	0.00078	1.15	5.02	2	1	1.5	2	1	0.06	1.6	0.4	1.7	1.7	2.55	5.1	10.12
1		SLEEVE	THERMOPLASTIC	INJ. MOULDING	A1	5600	0.00017	1.1	1	2	1	1	2	1	0.06	1.1	0.4	1.01	1.1	1.1	2.2	3.2

Figure 3.16   Comparison of pressure die casting and injection moulding processes for the manufacture of a critical surface finish

Comparison of alternative processing routes is illustrated in Figure 3.15. The impact extrusion and automatic machining process routes for the plug body design and production quantity requirements show significant manufacturing cost variation. The figure presents the detail of the cost analysis giving the values obtained from Pc and the individual elements involved in the calculation of Rc, together in the table with details of the design.

The benefits of the high material utilization associated with the impact extrusion process mean a large cost saving at the annual call-off of one million components. (The input volume for the machined component is almost five times that required for the impact extrusion.) However, as the annual production call-off reduces, the processing costs moves in favour of machining, and at a call-off of 20,000 per annum the sample data predicts little difference in cost between the two methods of production (see lower part of Figure 3.15).

A case where a material and process change eliminates the need for secondary processing is shown in Figure 3.16. An aluminium pressure die casting was used for the sleeve shown and secondary processing was needed to ensure conformance to surface finish requirements. The sample data does not differentiate between plastic injection moulding and pressure die casting in terms of basic processing cost. The savings indicated by the cost analysis result from lower material costs and surface finish capability of the injection moulding process reflected in Cft reduced from 1.7 to 1.1 (surface roughness for pressure die casting = 0.4–3.2 mm; injection moulding = 0.2–0.8 mm).

Adopting injection moulding here removes additional machining and minimizes the complexity of the manufacturing layout.

The technique can be helpful in producing cost estimates where design solutions involve a significant amount of sub-contract work. The estimates produced provide support to the make versus buy analysis and the technique can be useful in calibrating supplier quotations. (Variations of more than 30% in quotations from sub-contractors against identical specifications are common across the range of processes. This has been noted by a number of researchers over a number of years (3.14, 3.15).)

In this way benefits can be gained whether the methodology is applied as a stand-alone tool during product design/redesign or, more globally, as part of a company's integrated application of simultaneous engineering tools and techniques.

The applications of the methodology may be summarized as:

- determination of component cost in support of DFA
- competitor analysis
- assistance with make versus buy decisions
- cost estimating in concept design with low levels of component detail
- support for simultaneous engineering and team-work
- training in design for manufacture.

Computer support for enhancing the application of the methodology has been developed by CSC Manufacturing in the 'TeamSET' product and more information on this topic can be found in references (3.12, 3.13).

Concluding remarks

The need to provide the concept design and development stages of the product introduction process with carefully structured knowledge about process characteristics and capabilities, together with cost estimating methods has been highlighted.

Manufacturing process information maps (PRIMAs) of a standard form and similar level of detail for each manufacturing process have been presented. A simple method based on material and production quantity was designed to enable a user to focus attention on the most relevant manufacturing process. The application of the data provided in the PRIMAs as a means of selecting candidate manufacturing processes has been illustrated.

A method for costing of designs, that can be used from concept to detail, has been introduced. The novelty of the approach is the calculation of processing costs, based on the notion of design specific relative cost coefficients operating on cost – quantity maps giving costs for processing idealized designs.

Results of validation trails have indicated that the cost analysis can be used to predict component manufacturing costs, across a number of processes, to within 16% of actual values, using average process and material cost data. The performance of the analysis may be much improved through the use of company specific data.

The use of the PRIMAs and the design costing analysis with DFA provides a more holistic means of evaluating product designs and generating improved design solutions. In this way the wider application of DFA in industry is encouraged. In addition, the approach presented provides for the carrying out of structured competitor analysis and yields a means for investigating make versus buy decisions.

There are opportunities for the development of computer software to enhance the application of the process data and costing analysis. Potential benefits worth noting in this connection include: removal of error prone manual calculation and reference to maps and tables; consistency of results and standardized presentation; adherence to procedure; time saving; ease of editing and 'what if' exploration; peoples operation and improved version control.

Integration of computer-based process selection with other concurrent engineering software tools, such as DFA, also offers potential benefits. The machine facilitates improved management of information flow between the applications, and provides for common data entry, a shared database, reuse and control of data and traceability of decisions.

The CAD workstation provides additional scope for the application and integration of concurrent engineering software tools within the design process. Design information and outputs from application of the tools supplies useful input to the product modelling process.

The development of new and advanced materials and the continuous search for improved capability and lower processing costs means that process development is an important research issue in manufacturing engineering circles. Consequently the process selection problem is something of a moving target.

PRIMA development for standard processes not currently included and catering for new processes as they emerge is an activity where research effort is being placed. Also, feedback from users applying the work on new product development projects, including views on what additional data they would like to see included in the PRIMAs will provide a useful source of information for PRIMA development.

Similarly, user experience is being collected associated with application of the design costing analysis. Investigating the employment of business specific data in place of that provided for the sample set of processes included and the incorporation by companies of data on methods not in the set are other areas of research. In this way much more will be understood about ways of improving the analysis and its data, and the confidence that can be put on the resulting cost estimates.

Before leaving the topic of design costing it is worth saying that when costing designs the costs of non-conformance must always be considered. There is little point in saving a few pence or so on a component if attendant variability means rework, order exchange, warranty claims, etc. The costs of failure can totally swamp any pinched savings on manufacturing cost.

The intention behind the material presented here is to encourage the generation of capable design solutions and facilitate the exploration of their likely cost implications. Selection must not be based only on a minimum cost strategy. A 'quality first' strategy must be adopted.

Sample questions for students

The sample questions listed below provide some elemental ideas for examination questions and studies for students of engineering and business.

1. In a business concerned with product design and manufacture, why is it worth giving consideration to manufacturing process selection in the early stages of the design process?
2. What are the important criteria that influence process selection in a business? Consider both technological and economic issues. State which of the criteria defined, set limits on what can be achieved by the application of best practice in manufacturing operations.
3. Define a product introduction process and explain how it should be engineered to support the creation of products that are economic to manufacture?
4. Why have businesses implemented formal product introduction process models and how do these differ from the well established design process models?
5. Present an outline classification of engineering materials indicating the main categories and their subdivisions.
6. Define an outline classification of manufacturing processes indicating the main categories and their subdivisions.
7. Where does process selection fit in a methodology concerned with design for manufacture and assembly? Illustrate your answer with a simple flow chart.
8. Propose candidate material to process combinations for the following engineering components:
   (a) Cylinder head for an internal combustion engine
   (b) Spark plug body
   (c) Radar dish
   (d) 13 amp power plug body.
   Justify any selections made and limit your choice to a maximum of two candidates in each case.
9. Select three candidate methods for the manufacture of a low carbon steel tube, 20 mm diameter, 30 mm long with a uniform wall thickness of 2 mm. Rank each candidate for an annual production quantity of 10,000.
10. Why are zinc alloys commonly used for the manufacture of die cast components and give some typical examples?
11. The component shown in the figure below is to be manufactured by cold forming from a solid cylindrical slug of cold forming steel. Describe the main steps involved in man-

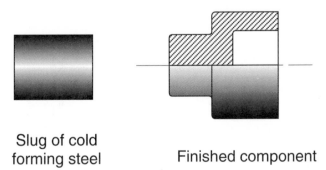

Slug of cold
forming steel   Finished component

ufacturing the part and comment on how the tooling would need to be proportioned to facilitate metal flow. Illustrate your answer with a sketch.

12. A mezzanine floor is to be fabricated from 1 m square, 5 mm thick low carbon steel panels. Propose methods for cutting the plate to size, preparing the edges, and welding the joints.

13. Compare injection moulding and pressure die casting for the manufacture of a small lightly loaded timer gear from a domestic appliance controller in terms of production rates and economics.

14. Contrast the manufacture of toothpaste tubes from aluminium and polymeric material.

15. Suggest suitable polymeric material and process combinations for the manufacture of the following components:
    (a) Cylindrical bottle (1 litre) for vegetable oil
    (b) Automobile handbrake lever
    (c) Computer casing
    (d) Automobile bumper.
    Justify any selections made and limit your selection to a maximum of two combinations in each case.

16. Compare the processing of metals and polymeric materials by continuous extrusion and explain the differences involved.

17. Contrast the application of adhesive bonding and spot welding for the assembly of pressed steel body panels in automobile manufacture.

18. Suggest suitable composite or ceramic material and process combinations for the manufacture of the following components:
    (a) Golf club heads and shafts
    (b) Aeroplane propeller blades
    (c) Metal cutting tool tips
    (d) High performance hydraulic pistons.
    Justify any selections made and limit yourself to a maximum of two combinations in each case.

19. In a writing a guide for advising the designer regarding injection and compression moulding, what design rules would you include and why?

20. Contrast the manufacture of piercing and blanking press tool dies by conventional machining/grinding, with electrical discharge machining.

21. Compare the production of machine tool stands or beds by fabrication techniques and sand casting in terms of economic and technical considerations.

22. The component illustrated in the following figure is to be manufactured by injection moulding unfilled PBT. Given that dimension 'A' is a customer critical characteristic to

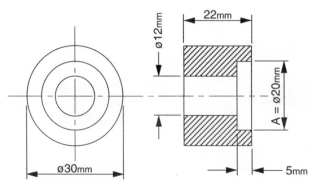

be maintained at $C_{pk} = 1.33$, estimate the cost of manufacture based on a production rate of 20,000 per annum.
(Answer: 7.8 pence.)

23. Suggest suitable methods for joining the components in the following assemblies:
    (a) A glass lens to the plastic moulded automobile headlamp
    (b) Alloy steel bicycle frame tube assembly
    (c) Heavy duty chain links for lifting equipment
    (d) Terminal posts and electronic components in printed circuit-boards.
    Justify the selections made and limit yourself to a maximum of two methods in each case.

24. Compare the production of phosphor bronze plain bearings by machining and powder metallurgy in terms of manufacturing economics and quality of conformance?

25. Contrast manually operated engine lathes, automatic lathes and CNC lathes in terms of manufacturing economics and technical capability?

26. The small aluminium alloy button shown in the figure below is currently produced by machining from solid bar at an annual production quantity of 60,000. Would an annual cost saving be possible if the part were to be made by pressure die casting?
    (Answers: Machined = 2.5 pence, Pressure die cast = 2.9 pence.)

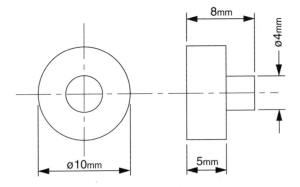

27. Construct process information maps (PRIMAs) for the following manufacturing processes:
    (a) Friction welding
    (b) Stereolithography
    (c) Superplastic forming
    (d) Diffusion bonding.

28. Collate and present component costing data that can be used with the costing analysis in Part III of this book for the following manufacturing processes:
    (a) Chemical milling
    (b) Compression moulding
    (c) Vacuum forming
    (d) Electrical discharge machining (EDM) processes.

29. Explain how you would use the process capability charts presented with the the PRIMAs in the tolerancing of component assemblies, and in liaison with suppliers?

30. What are the main criteria that influence the cost of a manufactured component? State which of the criteria are predetermined during the design process.

References

References – Part I

(1.1)	Chisolm, A. W. J. Design for Economic Manufacture, *Ann. CIRP*, 1973, **22**(2).
(1.2)	Bolz, R. W. *Production Processes: The Productivity Handbook*, 5th edn, Industrial Press Inc, New York, 1977.
(1.3)	Niebel, B. W., *Product Design and Process Engineering*, McGraw-Hill, 1974.
(1.4)	Rusinoff, S. E. *Manufacturing Processes: Materials and Production* 1962, American Technical Society.
(1.5)	Degarmo, E. P., Black, J. T. & Kohser, R. A., *Materials and Processes in Manufacturing*, 7th edn, Macmillan, New York, 1988.
(1.6)	Linberg, R. A., *Processes and Materials of Manufacture*, Allyn & Bacon, MA, 1983.
(1.7)	Boothroyd, G. & Dewhurst, P., *Product Design for Assembly*, Boothroyd Dewhurst Inc, Rhode Island, 1987.
(1.8)	Fume, A. & Knight, W. A., Computer based early cost estimating for sintered powder metal parts, *Proceedings of 4th International Conference on Product Design for Assembly*, Rhode Island, USA, June 1989.
(1.9)	Woodward, J. A. & Corbett, J., An expert system to assist the design for manufacture of die cast components, *Proceedings of 1989 International Conference on Engineering Design, (ICED89)*, Vol. II, Harrogate, UK, August 1989.
(1.10)	Shea, C., Reynolds, C. & Dewhurst, P., Computer aided material and process selection, *Proceedings of 4th International Conference on Product Design for Manufacture and Assembly*, Vol. I, Rhode Island, USA, June 1989.
(1.11)	Pighini, U., Long, W. & Todaro, F., Methodical Design for Manufacture, *Proceedings of 1989 International Conference on Engineering Design, (ICED89)*, Harrogate, UK, August 1989.
(1.12)	Zenger, D. C. & Boothroyd, G., Selection of manufacturing processes and materials for component parts, *Proceedings of 4th International Conference on Product Design for Manufacture and Assembly*, Rhode Island, June 1989.
(1.13)	Poli, C., Sunderland, J. E. & Fredette, L., Trimming the cost of die castings. *Machine Design*, March 8, 1990.
(1.14)	Allen, A. J. & Swift, K. G., Manufacturing process selection and costing, *Proc. Instn. Mech. Eng., Part B - Journal of Engineering Manufacture*, **204**, 1990.
(1.15)	Esawi, A. & Ashley, M. F., Cost estimation techniques for the early stages of design. Private communications, 1993.
(1.16)	Miles, B. L. & Swift, K. G., Working together. *Manufacturing Breakthrough*, March/April 1992.
(1.17)	Lucas Industries plc., Product Introduction Management, 1993.
(1.18)	Clausing, D. P., Quality function deployment, Mimeo report, February 1986.
(1.19)	Wood, D. and Croxall, S., Failure mode and effects analysis. *Conference on Tools and Techniques in Quality Engineering*, Manchester, October 1989.
(1.20)	Taguchi, G., *System of Experimental Design*, Vols 1/2, Kraus, New York 1987.
(1.21)	Johnson, T. G., (Chief Engineer), personal communication, Lucas Motors and Marine, 1994.
(1.22)	Boothroyd, G., Product design for manufacture and assembly. *Computer Aided Design*, July, **26**(7), 1994.
(1.23)	*Lucas DFA Practitioners Manual (Version 10.5)*, CSC Manufacturing, Solihull, 1996.
(1.24)	Boothroyd, G. & Dewhurst, P., *Product Design for Assembly*, Boothroyd Dewhurst Inc, Rhode Island, 1987.
(1.25)	Shimada, J., Design for manufacture, tools and methods: the Hitachi assemblability evaluation method (AEM), *Proceedings of 24th FISITA Congress*, London, 1992.
(1.26)	Boothroyd, G. & Dewhurst, P., Product design for manufacture and assembly. *Manufacturing Engineering*, pp. 42–46, April 1988.
(1.27)	Andreasen *et al.*, *Design for Assembly*, IFS Publication, UK, 1988.

(1.28) Boothroyd, G., Dewhurst, P. and Knight, W., *Product Design for Manufacture and Assembly*, Marcel Dekker, Inc., New York, 1994.

(1.29) Miles, B. L., Design for Assembly – A Key Element within Design for Manufacture. *Proc. Instn. Mech. Eng.*, **203**, 29–38, 1989.

(1.30) Kalpakjian, S., *Manufacturing Engineering and Technology*, 3rd edn, Addison Wesley, MA, 1995.

(1.31) Corbett *et al.*, *Design for Manufacture: Strategies, Principles and Techniques*, Addison Wesley, Bath, 1993.

(1.32) Schey, J., *Introduction to Manufacturing Processes*, 2nd edn, McGraw-Hill, 1987.

(1.33) Dieter, G., *Engineering Design: A Materials and Processing Approach*, 2nd edn, McGraw-Hill, 1991.

(1.34) Edwards, L. & Endean, M., *Manufacturing with Materials*, The Open University and Butterworths, 1992.

(1.35) Block, S. C., *Principles of Engineering Manufacture*, Arnold, London, 1996.

(1.36) Plunkett, J. J. & Dale, B. G., *Quality Costing*, Chapman & Hall, London, 1991.

References – Part II

(2.1) Field, S. W. & Swift, K. G., *Effecting a Quality Change*, Arnold, London, 1996.

(2.2) Batchelor, R. and Swift, K. G. Conformability analysis in support of design for quality. *Proc. Instn. Mech. Eng.*, **210**, 37–47, 1996.

(2.3) Swift, K. G. & Booker, J. D., Engineering for Conformance, *The TQM Magazine*, **8**(3), 54–60, 1996.

(2.4) Swift, K. G. & Booker, J. D., *Conformability Analysis Workbook – Version 1.0*, University of Hull, 1997 (to be published).

References – Part III

(3.1) Pugh, S., *Cost Information for the Designer*, First National Design Conference, London, 1977.

(3.2) Farag, M. M., *Selection of Materials and Manufacturing Processes for Engineering Design*, Prentice Hall, Hemel Hempstead, 1989.

(3.3) Hundal, M. S., *Cost Models for Product Design*. ICED '93, The Hague, 17–19 August, 1993.

(3.4) Allen, A. J. & Swift, K. G., Manufacturing process selection and costing. *Proc. Instn. Mech. Eng.*, **203**, 1990.

(3.5) Allen, A. J., *et al*, Development of a Manufacturing analysis and costing system. *Int. J. Adv. Manuf. Tech.*, **6**, 205–215, 1991.

(3.6) Braund, R. Manufacturability analysis – assessing the effects of component size on processing costs. Research Report, Department of Engineering Design and Manufacture, University of Hull, 1995.

(3.7) Hammond, S., personal communication, A. T. Poeton Ltd., 1994.

(3.8) Ashby, M. F., *Materials Selection in Mechanical Design*, Pergamon Press Ltd, Oxford, 1992.

(3.9) Waterman, N. A., Computer Based Materials Selection Systems. *Metals and Materials*, **8**(1),19–24, 1992.

(3.10) Crane, F. A. A. & Charles, J. A., *Selection and Use of Engineering Materials*, Butterworth, London, 1984.

(3.11) Hird, G., personal communication. Lucas Industries Ltd., 1994.

(3.12) Sealy, M., Berriman, P. & Marti, Y-M, A practical solution for implementing sustainable improvements in product introduction performance. *1992 FISITA Conference*.

(3.13) TeamSET Software Manual. CSC Manufacturing, Solihull, 1996.

(3.14) Gallagher, C. C. & Southern G., Classification – the answer to consistent job estimates and quotations. *Machinery Production Engineering*, January 1973, No. 131.

(3.15) Lenau, T., *et al.*, Design for pressure die casting – a DFM example. *Int. J. Adv. Manuf. Tech.*, **6**, 141–154, 1991.

Bibliography

Dallas, D. B. *et al.*, *Tool and Manufacturing Engineers Handbook*, 3rd Edition, Society of Manufacturing Engineers, McGraw-Hill, New York, 1976.

Green, R. E. (ed), *Machinery's Handbook*, 24th edn, Industrial Press Inc., New York, 1992.

Bolz, R. W., *Production Processes: The Productivity Handbook*, 5th edn, Industrial Press Inc, New York, 1977.

Degarmo, E. P., Black, J. T. & Kohser, R. A., *Materials and Processes in Manufacturing*, 7th edn, Macmillan, New York, 1988.

Linberg, R. A., *Processes and Materials of Manufacture*, Allyn and Bacon, MA, 1983.

Kalpakjian, S., *Manufacturing Engineering and Technology*, 3rd edn, Addison Wesley, MA, 1995.

Schey, J., *Introduction to Manufacturing Processes*, 2nd edn, McGraw-Hill, 1987.

Waterman, N. A. & Ashby, M. F. (eds.), *Elsevier Materials Selector*, Elsevier Science Publishers, Essex, 1991.

Ashby, M. F., *Materials Selection in Mechanical Design*, Pergamon Press, Oxford, 1992.

Index